Show Don't Tell
The Ultimate Writers' Guide

Robyn Opie Parnell

Show Don't Tell: The Ultimate Writers' Guide

Copyright © 2014 Robyn Opie Parnell

Cover Design: fiverr.com/ilgeorgiev

An Я&R Production
PO Box 485
Morphett Vale SA 5162
Australia
http://www. rnrbooksfilmmusic.com.au
info@rnrbooksfilmmusic.com.au

DEDICATION

To my darling husband and soul mate, Rob Parnell.

CONTENTS

ACKNOWLEDGMENTS

A special thanks to the authors whose extracts have been included in this writers' resource. *The moral rights of the authors have been asserted.*

© King, Stephen, *Cujo*, Viking Press, 1981
© Brown, Dan, *Inferno*, Doubleday, 2013
© Martin, George R. R., *Game of Thrones*, Bantam Books, 1996
© Picoult, Jodi, *The Storyteller*, Atria Books, 2013
© Patterson, James, *Four Blind Mice*, Little, Brown and Company, 2002
© Anderson, Natalie, *Blame It On The Bikini*, Harlequin Mills & Boon, 2013
© Koontz, Dean, *Frankenstein: City of Night*, HarperCollins Publishers, 2005
© Pemberton, Lynne, *Dancing With Shadows*, HarperCollins Publishers, 1998
© Patterson, James, *Violets are Blue*, Little, Brown, 2001
© James, E. L., *Fifty Shades of Grey*, Random House, 2012
© Hill, Joe, *Murder Past Midnight*, Origin Books, 2013
© Collins, Suzanne, *The Hunger Games*, Scholastic Inc., 2008
© Young, William P., *The Shack*, Windblown Media, 2007
© Harris, Thomas, *The Silence of the Lambs*, St. Martin's Press, 1988
© Lehane, Dennis, *Sacred*, Bantam Books, 2006
© Patterson James, *Alex Cross, Run*, Grand Central Publishing, 2013
© Probst, Jennifer, *Executive Seduction*, Cool Gus Publishing, 2013
© Fielding, Helen, *Bridget Jones's Diary*, Picador, 1996
© Dostoyevsky, Fyodor, *Crime and Punishment*, Russian Messenger, 1866
© Sebold, Alice, *The Lovely Bones*, Little, Brown, 2002
© Higgins, Jack, *The Eagle Has Landed*, Collins, 1975
© Meyer, Stephenie, *Twilight*, Little, Brown Books for Young Readers, 2005
© Rowling, J. K., *Harry Potter and the Sorcerer's Stone*, Bloomsbury, 1997
© Brown, Dan, *The Da Vinci Code*, Doubleday, 2003
© Baker, Madeline, *Warrior's Lady*, Leisure Books, 1993

Why You Should Read This Book

Hi, I'm Robyn Opie Parnell.

A few years ago, I was a judge in a contest for new writers. Over a one-month period, I was asked to read numerous contest entries, all of which were children's stories. Amongst the entries was a handful of great stories that really stood out. These gems were different in style and genre. They were aimed at different age groups. But they all had one thing in common. The authors knew how to hook readers through their skillful use of *show, don't tell*.

The first entry I read was hard to put down. In the early hours of the morning, I forced myself to stop reading and turn off the light. I didn't want to go to sleep. I wanted to stay awake and keep reading. But people need sleep, my tired husband reminded me.

When I finished reading the story, a day or two later, I wanted to continue with the next installment. The entry was the first in a series and, at the end of book one, I was ready for more. I needed more. I didn't want to leave this fictional world and its characters. Clearly the other judges had similar reactions because this entry went on to win the Grand Prize.

A few entries later, I sat in my living room reading a Young Adult manuscript. Again, I wanted to read until I finished the story. I was so engrossed, I didn't want to stop, and I'm not too proud to admit that this particular entry made me cry. It was an emotional journey which I thoroughly enjoyed. As the story concluded, I felt a sense of loss, as if I was saying goodbye to dear friends. The other judges must have enjoyed this story, too, because this entry won First Prize.

The entries which won Second Prize and Honorable Mention were also favorites of mine. In fact, the judges didn't have any trouble agreeing on the top four entries. Without consultation, we came up with the same list of winners. Our easy agreement was further evidence that *show, don't tell* is the key to winning contests and the hearts of readers.

On the flipside, the entries which I and the other judges enjoyed the least also had one thing in common. They were all *telling* and, too often, from the point of view of an adult narrator. They were children's stories. Why was an adult *telling* them?

I was pleased to have my thoughts on *show, don't tell* validated by the contest. The winning stories all involved *showing* from the main character's point of view. The stories which were never in the race all involved *telling* and, too often, from the point of view of an adult narrator.

Over the years, I've realized that many people are *telling* stories, rather than *showing* their readers what is happening in scenes of movement. I've read some interesting stories from new writers but they are little more than a series of events i.e. this happened, then this, then this etc.

These stories are more like plot outlines or synopses rather than novels. They have potential. Each story can be improved if the writer opts for a *showing* rather than a *telling* style.

Why is *showing* from the main character's point of view so

important? Why do the best stories involve *showing* and not *telling*?

The answers to these questions are easy if you consider my reactions to the winning entries in the contest for new writers.

When a writer *shows* a story from the main character's point of view, the story is often hard to put down. Readers experience the story, as if they are the main character, as if the events are happening to them. Readers see, hear, think and feel everything the main character does. If the main character is saddened by the tragic death of a friend so, too, are the readers.

The scenes in a book are like those in a movie. However, in a book, the writer uses words to create scenes in the minds of readers by engaging their imaginations. Readers participate because *showing* requires them to use their imaginations to work out what is going on. *Showing* requires readers to participate by using their imaginations to come to their own conclusions based on the writer's words. Writers are not *telling* readers. Readers are being *shown* what is going on and are pulled into the story because they have to interpret the writer's meaning themselves.

Doesn't this sound like real life? In real life, we see and hear scenes, and we have to interpret them ourselves. Most of us don't have a narrator who *tells* us what is going on in our daily lives. We have to make up our own minds, given what we see and hear.

When we interpret information ourselves, we bring our own experiences and personalities to a story. We add to the story and make it our own. We personalize it. We know how we'd feel in similar situations, and we bring these thoughts and feelings to the story. Through this participation, we're drawn or pulled into the story. We're involved.

The most important aspect of *show, don't tell* is that *showing* makes readers care. Why do we care? Because we're involved, we're participating. When we're involved and participating, what happens matters to us. Events and their outcomes make a difference to us. They affect us. Yes, we care.

Telling, on the other hand, does not engage the imagination. We're told something – a statement of fact, a foregone conclusion. We cannot see, hear, feel or think about the words. We cannot add to them. The writer is *telling* us something. The writer has made the decision for us. There is no interpretation on our behalf. No argument. No participation for readers. No involvement. We're kept outside the story, at a distance. And we have no choice but to accept what the writer says as gospel. But do we?

No. We like to make up our own minds. We like proof which we can interpret and understand. Why should we simply believe the writer? We don't even know him!

Let's look at an example: *He was scared.* Sorry, but this means nothing to me. So what? Who cares? I don't feel anything. The word *scared* doesn't make me scared. I can't see, hear, think or feel anything. I'm not involved or participating. I can't bring my own experiences and personality to these three words. I can't relate. Besides, how do I know that he was scared? What proof do I have? Am I supposed to just accept this statement without question?

Now, if I *show* this scene: *He listened. All he could hear was his pounding heart and ragged breathing. He held his breath, trying to still his body, so he could hear other noises. Silence greeted his ears, with an undertone of his pounding heart and ragged breathing. Damn! What about the killer? Had the killer followed him? As far as he could tell he was alone. For now. God! He had no choice. He had to breathe; slowly, carefully, silently. His forehead was damp with sweat but he didn't dare wipe the dampness away.*

The above scene was off the top of my head, so please forgive me if it's not my best writing. The point is that this *showing* scene involves readers. It gives readers a chance to interpret the words, to come to their own conclusions and, most importantly, to put themselves in the main character's shoes. Readers can imagine how they'd feel in the same situation. Readers can imagine what they'd do, how they'd react. Readers can experience the fear without being there, without being in danger. Readers can live vicariously through the main character – and they do. Readers also believe in this fictional world. They have reasons to believe in the main character's fear. They have proof. The main character's physical and emotional reactions offer evidence, as do his thoughts about the killer. There's no doubt that we'd experience similar reactions if in his position. Actually, I might not be as together as my main character.

He was scared doesn't cut it. We can't imagine it. For one thing, there isn't enough information for us to engage our imaginations. *Scared* doesn't mean much to us. But the emotions, thoughts and physical reactions of fear do. We've all experienced them at one time or another.

As a writer, one of your main purposes – if not the main one – is to elicit emotions in your readers. If you don't elicit emotions, how can you expect your readers to care? Why should they keep reading your story or book? To elicit emotions, you need to engage your readers' imaginations and emotions. Just saying *he was scared* is not enough, not by a long shot.

When you write, you need to *show* your readers the emotions, thoughts and physical reactions of your main character. Let your readers experience what your main character does, as if your readers are the main character. Think about why we read – for escapism. And let your readers escape into your stories through involvement and participation, through identification and connection.

In *Show Don't Tell: the Ultimate Writers' Guide*, I plan to *show* you how to write fiction that grabs your readers, that gives them a most satisfying experience, that makes them forget their own world and that makes them want to keep reading about your fictional world until the very last page of your book.

In *Show Don't Tell: the Ultimate Writers' Guide*, I cover in detail:

1. **Show, Don't Tell – What It Is and How It Works**

2. **Show, Don't Tell and the Various Genres**

3. **Show, Don't Tell and Characters**

4. **Show, Don't Tell Supplemental**

5. **Show, Don't Tell and Dialogue**

6. **Show, Don't Tell and Conflict**

7. **Show, Don't Tell and Plot Progression**

8. **Show, Don't Tell and Short Stories**

9. **Show, Don't Tell and Editing**

10. **Show, Don't Tell Bonus**

Many writers say that they understand the techniques of *show, don't tell*. But do they?

In this ultimate writers' guide, we're going to look at *show, don't tell* in relation to every aspect of novel or short story writing. We'll look at creating conflict and tension, forwarding the plot, building believable characters and using realistic dialogue – plus more.

Yes, I'm sure you've studied these elements of writing in the past, on the road to becoming your best possible writer. But this time, you'll consider these important elements from the point of view of *show, don't tell.*

We'll look at how best selling writers use *showing* to hook their readers from beginning to end. You'll do exercises to enhance your own *show, don't tell* skills. You'll be able to look at your work and maximize the effect your writing has on your readers.

At the end, you'll have a thorough knowledge and comprehensive notes on *show, don't tell* – what it means, how it works and why it's important.

You'll be able to use this new knowledge to improve your writing and give yourself an advantage when submitting to publishers. Let's face it, an editor will show preference for a professionally written manuscript, containing every ingredient possible. This ultimate writers' guide will assist you in maximizing your chances of publishing success.

Show, don't tell is not a skill that comes easily to many writers. But it is a skill that can be learned. It's possible to give your writing new life and turn a tired, passive voice into a fresh, active voice.

If you learn the principles of *show, don't tell*, you, too, can win contests and the hearts of your readers.

1

Show, Don't Tell – What It Is and

How It Works

Let me *show* you what I mean by *show, don't tell* by considering the visual art of making movies.

A movie is made up of scenes. These scenes allow the audience to get inside the story and get to know the characters.

Imagine you're a movie director and your job is to create compelling images necessary to draw your audience into the story.

A movie director doesn't have the luxury of *telling* the audience that a character is scared.

The director has to find a way to *show* the audience what is going on through characters' physical reactions, body language, dialogue or interchange between characters and situations.

Obviously a director uses images on a screen to invoke a prescribed response – to elicit emotions – from the viewing audience.

If you watch a horror movie, the director wants you to feel scared – horrified, even. If you watch a romance, the director wants you to feel love, happiness and hope for the future. If you watch a drama, the director wants you to feel the drama.

As a writer, your job should be to create images within your readers' minds that invoke a prescribed response from your readers i.e. which elicit emotions. You want your readers to feel the emotions your characters experience during each situation or scene. The difference is that you're using words, and not film, to create the images.

Therefore, a book is also made up of scenes, which allow the readers to get inside the story and get to know the characters.

Showing is the tool writers use to pull readers into a scene. *Showing* creates a bond between the readers and the scene/characters. *Showing* draws readers into your story as they interpret what is going on. *Showing* involves readers by engaging their imaginations and allowing them to participate by adding their own backgrounds, personalities and experiences to the scene. *Showing* causes readers to identify with and relate to the main character.

Telling keeps readers outside. *Telling* distances readers. *Telling* makes readers back away.

Let's say that your aim is to elicit the emotion of fear in your readers. If you write *Donna was scared*, this sort of *telling* leaves no room for readers' personal interpretation or improvisation. The imagination is uninvolved. There's nothing for readers to do. There's nothing readers can add to this statement. It's a foregone conclusion. Finito! The writer has made the decision for readers. However, when you – the writer – *show* that the character is scared through action and physical responses, you involve the imagination and allow your readers' minds free range to interpret your words.

Here are some examples of *telling*:

- She felt tired.

- He was worried.

- It was stormy.

Here are the same examples using *show* instead of *tell*:

- She fell into a chair. Her feet ached and she thought about removing her shoes but she couldn't muster the energy.

- He closed his eyes, frowned and rubbed his forehead. What was he going to do?

- He looked out the kitchen window. Rain splattered against the glass and drilled a staccato beat on the iron roof. Thunder crashed overhead. His dog whined.

And so on.

Personally, I prefer the second *showing* examples. They get me more involved in the story and characters' lives because I have to read the words and work out what is going on. I'm involved. I'm participating. To be involved and participating, I must be drawn into the story and characters. These *showing* scenes are more entertaining than their poor *telling* cousins.

As you can see from the above examples, *showing* often provides readers with more information in a subtle way that doesn't appear as if character or background information is being added. For example, we now know that the man looking out his kitchen window into the stormy weather has a dog.

And what if I changed the second example to: *He closed his eyes, frowned and rubbed the smooth scalp of this bald head. What was he going to do?*

Now we know that the worried man is bald. I've added a little character description without being obvious or slowing down the story.

Showing often does more than one thing. *Showing* adds to plot or conflict or characterization. *Showing* moves a story forward.

Let's look at an example of *showing* from Stephen King's novel *Cujo*:

And then the growling began.

His heart leaped into his throat and he fell back a step, all his muscles tensing into bundles of wire. His first panicky thought, like a child who has suddenly tumbled into a fairy tale, was wolf, and he looked around wildly. There was nothing to see but white.

Cujo came out of the fog.

Now, I'm going to upset Mr. King and rewrite the above lines in a *telling* style. My apologies to Mr. King.

And then the growling began.

He was frightened. He was tense. He looked around. There was nothing to see but white.

Cujo came out of the fog.

My second example is okay. But Stephen King's original is much better than mine because he shows the character's fear through action, physical reactions and thoughts. Stephen King builds the drama and tension before adding the wonderful words, *Cujo came out of the fog.*

In my *telling* rewrite, there isn't enough build-up of drama and tension. One of the reasons is that readers don't get a true sense of the character's fear and therefore don't experience the fear as if in the character's shoes. Readers don't know how frightening this experience really is for the character. The impact or importance of this scene is lost as the fear is diluted by my *telling* style. In my version, the final words in this scene – *Cujo came out of the fog* – are almost a "so what?" moment. Who cares?

People read for escapism. They want to be transported into a story, to share the characters' emotions and experiences. They want to feel the horror and fear from the safety of their homes, offices, trains, parks etc. It's the fly on the wall scenario. You can imagine the reader saying, "This is fantastic, as long as it isn't really happening to me."

Stephen King's (*showing*) scene does all of that. The carefully chosen words pull readers into the story and get them involved. Readers know that the character is frightened without being told that he is frightened. His actions are those of a scared man. Readers are given enough information to draw their own conclusions, to feel like a fly on the wall watching and interpreting the scene just as in real life. Readers believe what is happening because they make their own assumptions from the information they're given.

The author has trusted readers to recreate the scene from within their own minds. Readers' imaginations conjure pictures of the characters acting, reacting, thinking etc. The writer shouldn't intrude on the story by *telling* readers what they should imagine. The author should be the *invisible* aspect of any good book.

Showing is active, as opposed to passive. This means that a writer should use dialogue, action, description, thoughts and feelings to create scenes of movement.

Readers are less likely to become bored or distracted when they are involved in the story.

Can you remember times when you didn't want to put a book down? The writer had you caught up in the story. The writer was *showing* you enough to keep you hooked, by means of either plot or action or conflict – or combinations of all these and more.

My rewritten (*telling*) version *tells* us that the character is frightened. We are being lectured or hit over the head with a sledgehammer. The scene fails to get us involved in the story.

No one likes to be told how to think or feel. So why would you do this to your readers?

Telling is passive. Sure, we understand what's going on. However, the picture in our minds (if we even have a picture) is unremarkable and fails to stir our emotions. "So what? Who cares?" are the words that pop into our heads.

Showing is necessary in horror especially to create tension and evoke emotional responses from readers. Fear. Horror. Disgust. *Showing* is necessary to make readers identify with and care about your characters.

Another word for *showing* is *dramatization*.

Here's another example of *showing* from *Inferno* by Dan Brown:

Langdon bolted awake, shouting.

The room was bright. He was alone. The sharp smell of medicinal alcohol hung in the air, and somewhere a machine pinged in quiet rhythm with his heart. Langdon tried to move his right arm, but a sharp pain restrained him. He looked down and saw an IV tugging at the skin of his forearm.

His pulse quickened, and the machines kept pace, pinging more rapidly.

Where am I? What happened?

Dan Brown could have *told* us:

Langdon bolted awake, shouting.

He was in a hospital and he had no idea how he got there.

Now I know which scene I prefer. The first version pulls me into the story. As a reader, I have the same information as the main character, Langdon. Initially, I don't know where Langdon is but as he describes his surroundings, I can interpret where he is, though I'm not sure what is going on. The first version makes me ask questions or want to know more i.e. it makes me want to turn the pages. Okay, the second version makes me curious too. But it doesn't have the same impact. The second version keeps me outside of the story – distant. Again, with the second version, there's a sense of "so what?" and "who cares?" because the writer didn't take enough time and care to draw readers into her fictional world.

We're talking about the difference between an average book and a best seller.

Showing is necessary in thrillers to create tension and suspense, to keep the reader guessing and wanting to know more.

So, is *showing* better than *telling*?

A lot of the time it is, but not always. Some *telling* is necessary to a story. This is most commonly labeled *narration* or *exposition*. The writer needs to *tell* readers some aspects of what is happening, or sometimes may need to add background details to help the readers build visual mental images.

Here is an example of *telling* from Dan Brown's *Inferno*:

He had always enjoyed the solitude and independence provided him by his chosen life of bachelorhood, although he had to admit, in his current situation, he'd prefer to have a familiar face at his side.

In the above example, Dan Brown initially *tells* readers that

Langdon has always enjoyed his chosen life of bachelorhood and why. But then Dan Brown skillfully *shows* readers how Langdon feels about bachelorhood at this point in the story.

A little *telling* adds to characterization. However, Dan Brown wisely reverts to *showing* as soon as he possibly can. Dan Brown wants readers to identify and sympathize with Robert Langdon, and he uses the techniques of *show, don't tell* to do so.

Telling (or narrative) is a good way to slow down the pace of any story. During passages of narration, the readers' minds are given a short reprieve from constant action.

Let's face it, readers don't want to have their emotions evoked for the duration of a 400-page novel. That would be incredibly exhausting.

Telling is your best choice when you want to summarize something like background history, such as Langdon's chosen life of bachelorhood, or for smooth transitions between scenes. *Tell* when you need to back away, to keep readers at a distance. For instance, using a *telling* style when introducing murderers or bad guys will stop your readers from identifying and sympathizing with the nemesis.

We'll discuss when to use a *telling* style in more detail as we journey through this guide.

Showing is your best choice when you want readers to be emotionally involved in your fictional world. Revealing the action and emotion via *showing* scenes makes your story memorable in readers' minds, whereas *telling* readers how to think and feel, thus removing any engagement of their imaginations, makes your story fade into the background.

Telling a scene is often easier than *showing* a scene. As a writer, you should work harder to find ways of bringing a piece to life that draw readers into your world and don't let go.

Now it's over to you.

The following are activities I suggest you complete to enhance and intensify your learning experience. These activities are intended to get you studying and questioning the techniques of *show, don't tell*.

Pick out a novel you remember as being particularly enthralling. Flip through the pages and find at least one example of *showing* and one of *telling*.

Is that author's style one of *showing* or *telling* – or a careful combination of both?

Can you see why certain passages drew you into the story and which pieces your eyes glossed over? Did these passages contain examples of *showing* or *telling*? How did you feel as you read each piece? What is the author trying to *show* in each piece? Could the author have used *showing* instead of *telling* in parts – and vice versa?

2

Show, Don't Tell and the Various

Genres

In the last module, we looked at s*how, don't tell* — what it is and how it works.

To recap, *showing* is about involving a reader in your story — as if he/she is watching events unfold, like a fly on the wall. *Showing* allows your reader to participate by interpreting your words and adding his/her own personality and experiences to the story. *Showing* is about bringing the reader in close to the story and characters so that he/she cares about the unfolding events. If your reader doesn't care, what's stopping him/her from watching a movie?

Telling has its place. A little *telling* can be useful. In fact, a great novel is a blend of *showing* and *telling* – with the writer *showing* approximately 85 to 90 per cent of the time. The masters know how to use both *showing* and *telling* to their advantage.

Telling distances the reader. *Telling* is useful when you want a reader to scan over information i.e. when you do not want to elicit an emotional response from your reader.

Now we're going to look at *show, don't tell* and the various genres.

Let's start with the genres of science fiction and fantasy.

With science fiction and fantasy, you want to draw readers deep into your fictional world. You have to convince readers that your impossible scenario is not only plausible but is a reality for the universe you've created. This is called *suspension of disbelief.*

Has a friend ever told you a story that's left you feeling skeptical and disbelieving? If the same friend had evidence to support the tale, you would have little trouble believing it – even if the story still sounds outrageous.

The easiest way to convince someone of something is to *show* him or her. In other words, to *show* them proof.

Imagine you're watching an episode of *Star Trek* – your favorite television series. Now imagine that you're listening to the same episode on a radio. Which will be the most convincing – watching the television show or listening to the radio broadcast?

My answer is: watching the television show.

Why?

Because television allows us to see what's taking place, to witness events as if we're there. This visual medium makes it easier for us to believe in what we're seeing as real events in real worlds with real people.

I keep referring to film and television because they rely on images to convey a story.

And so do books.

Showing is about creating images in readers' minds.

Readers want vivid images in their heads. They want to believe a writer's imaginary events. Otherwise, they wouldn't pick up a book. They want to experience the story as if they are there, but safely away from any horrors and dangers. The pages of a book offer escapism for readers.

It isn't enough to *tell* readers. Writers need to convince readers that their fictional worlds are real. Writers have to provide evidence — to *show* readers.

So *showing* is about:

1. Convincing readers that a fictional world is real;

2. Making readers care about the main character and his/her problem;

3. Evoking readers' emotions; and

4. Allowing readers to participate and interpret scenes for themselves.

Readers are more likely to believe your story if they have to work things out for themselves. Get their imaginations working overtime. *Show* them that your characters are not perturbed by the unusual settings or circumstances around them. In fact, the more acceptance you can *show* each character portraying for the fantastical elements in their world, the more believable it becomes to your readers.

The following example is from George R. R. Martin's *Game of Thrones*:

The Other slid forward on silent feet. In its hand was a longsword like none that Will had ever seen. No human metal had gone into the forging of that blade. It was alive with moonlight, translucent, a shard of crystal so thin that it seemed almost to vanish when seen edge-on. There was a faint blue shimmer to the thing, a ghost-light that played around its edges, and somehow Will knew that it was sharper than any razor.

This scene is fantasy – pure fiction. At the same time, this scene is convincing because it comes from the character's point of view. It's like hearing witness testimony. Will describes what he sees and believes to be true. He adds his own interpretations and experiences to what he witnesses. It's difficult to argue with descriptions that come from an eye witness, even a fictional one.

Readers can put themselves in Will's shoes and picture the scene in their own minds, thanks to George R. R. Martin's descriptions. Readers might not know Will's world but they know enough to transpose their own experiences for Will's.

If you *tell* readers about the unusual circumstances surrounding your characters and their world, readers may not believe you. If you *show* readers scenes in which your characters act as eye witnesses, readers are more inclined to believe in the fictional "reality" because your characters offer proof by way of descriptions of what they're seeing, hearing, touching, tasting, smelling, thinking and feeling.

Now let's look at the genres of mystery, crime and thriller.

Here's an example from *The Storyteller* by Jodi Picoult:

Jocelyn raises her hand. "I have a real problem with that."

I blush even deeper, assuming she's talking about me, but then I realize that she's staring at the urn in Mrs. Dombrowski's lap.

"It's disgusting!" Jocelyn says. "We weren't supposed to bring something dead. We were supposed to bring a memory."

Readers want to see the drama in their heads – vividly. This example *shows* us what Jocelyn is feeling through her actions and dialogue. Readers also learn how Sage (the main character) reacts and feels through her body language and thoughts. We gain an insight into Sage's character – she thinks that Jocelyn is talking about her – so the scene adds to characterization. Plus, this scene suggests that trouble is brewing. It moves the plot forward. It's page-turning magic.

Do we care that trouble is around the corner for Sage or her grief therapy group?

Not yet, because this scene is in the first few pages of the novel. But it creates interest, intrigue, and is supposed to make us want to know more. It works for me.

Here's a scene from James Patterson's *Four Blind Mice*:

Tanya Jackson opened the kitchen door and looked terribly confused for a split second, before Thomas Sharkey cut her throat with the survival knife. The woman moaned, dropped to her knees, then fell onto the floor. Tanya was dead before she hit the black and olive-green checkerboard linoleum of the kitchen floor.

"Somebody's very good with a survival knife. You haven't lost your touch over the years," Harris said to Sharkey as he drank beer and watched the movie.

I admit that James Patterson *tells* us how Tanya Jackson looks – terribly confused. James Patterson also *shows* the scene with such concise, tight writing that he creates an almost clinical coldness to murder, which is the point surely. Murder is cold.

The scene is made much more powerful because James Patterson then *shows* us clearly that the murderers are seasoned, hardened professionals without a hint of conscience between them by using one simple line of dialogue and action. These people murder with ease, so much so that immediately afterwards they drink a beer and watch a movie.

Tanya's murder is deliberately concise and tight, because James Patterson is more concerned with painting a picture of the murderers and making the reader feel revulsion for them rather than sympathy for Tanya. She's just another victim.

James Patterson knew exactly what he wanted his readers to feel when he wrote this passage. His words were no accident. They were carefully chosen. Tanya has little relevance to the story, except as a tool to provide an insight into the murderers and create sympathy or fear for the hero who has to stop them.

James Patterson could have *told* us that the murderers are cold-hearted brutes who kill with no conscience or remorse. I think most of us know that, anyway, without being told. James Patterson *shows* us the cold-hearted brutes with no conscience or remorse because he wants us to feel the emotions, as if we are part of this story. He wants to drag us into his fictional world and he doesn't want us to leave until we've read the very last word.

In a mystery, crime or thriller, readers get to picture each plot element unfolding. We want to be *shown* clues and sometimes red herrings. We want to participate and guess at the killer or the outcome. Some of us want to be ahead of the detective or crime-solving main character.

We want to experience and feel the excitement, action, adventure, fear, or disgust.

We want to catch the bad guys from the safety and comfort of our homes, buses, trains or bathtubs.

We want *showing* to evoke our imaginations.

Now let's look at another genre – romance.

Readers enjoy romance novels for a sense of escapism. Our daily existences can be unromantic, especially if we're single (or maybe that should read – especially if we're married).

Most of us have experienced romance and love at some point in our lives. Maybe the romance or love has faded. Sometimes it becomes jaded and vanishes altogether. But we can remember the strong feelings, the natural highs. So we bring our personalities and experiences to a romantic story.

Some romances are intended to be quick reads. Just as

chocolate can give us a quick sugar fix, some books can give us a quick romance fix.

The following example is from a Mills & Boon romance *Blame It On The Bikini* written by Natalie Anderson.

Topping the modelicious height, his dark brown hair was neatly trimmed, giving him a clean-cut, good-boy look. He was anything but good. Then there were the eyes—light brown maple-syrup eyes, with that irresistible golden tinge to them. With a single look that he'd perfected at an eyebrow-raising young age, he could get any woman to beg him to pour it over her.

And Brad obliged. The guy had had more girlfriends than Mya had worked overtime hours.

In the above example, Natalie Anderson describes Brad from the main character's point of view. Readers see how Brad looks through Mya's eyes and they get a hint of his personality through Mya's thoughts. Natalie Anderson's words create pictures in readers' minds. Readers experience events as if they are in Mya's shoes. Readers react as they interpret the words, based on their own backgrounds, personalities and experiences.

At best, romance can take a reader to that happy place where perfect endings are guaranteed and the girl inevitably gets her ideal man. At worst, however…

Let's look at another example. This time from Madeline Baker's *Warrior's Lady*:

Sometimes they used him for target practice, making him run the length of the long, narrow corridor outside his chamber while they hurled rocks at him. Sometimes, when they had no wish to play, they let Gar whip him a few times, then they tied him by his wrists and left him hanging from the rafters like the carcass of some dead animal while they played cards in a corner of the room, not caring that the shallow cuts ached unceasingly, that great horned flies came to bite him, gorging themselves on his blood, not caring that the quivering muscles in his arms and shoulders screamed for relief.

The above excerpt is a prime example of *over-telling*. The reader is not drawn into any plot progression, nor is the reader learning much about the central character except that he has been tortured at some point in the past. This entire paragraph was *told* as a flashback – a memory from the past. No new conflict or action was introduced into the scene to heighten tension. In other words, the author has not *shown* us any real reason to keep turning the pages.

Let's face it – this is a romance novel. Where in this passage is the reader drawn into the sweeping emotions involved with a love story?

Imagine how differently we might have felt if we'd been drawn into the harsh emotions involved with being tortured. The author could have *shown* us instead how the poor protagonist dealt with the difficult emotions he had to overcome before trusting the book's heroine and falling in love. Instead, we are *told* about the situation from his past and *told* how hard it was for him. The reader has no chance to emote with the protagonist's plight at all.

The emotion is diffused and the tension is subdued by the very act of *over-telling* instead of *showing*.

Ah, now to horror...

I mentioned horror in the first module and used an example from Stephen King's *Cujo*. Now I'd like to use a short piece from *Frankenstein: City of Night* by Dean Koontz.

Showered, feeling pretty in a summery dress of yellow silk, Erika left the master suite to explore the mansion. She felt like the unnamed narrator and heroine of Rebecca, for the first time touring the lovely rooms of Manderley.

In the upstairs hall, she found William, the butler, on his knees in a corner, chewing off his fingers one by one.

Horror disturbs us. And not because we've been *told* something horrible. But because the writer has created realistic, believable images in our minds, with the purpose of engaging our imaginations and emotions. It's almost like the writer gets inside us and uses our emotions against us.

One of the reasons I chose the above example from Dean Koontz is because of the contrast between the two paragraphs. Readers picture Erika exploring the mansion, while feeling pretty in her yellow silk summery dress. As we picture Erika, we're reminded of the novel *Rebecca*. Then we're confronted by William, the butler, on his knees in a corner, chewing off his fingers one by one. The contrast is shocking. The image of William is simple, yet disturbing. Coming at the end of chapter 8, these two paragraphs are definitely page-turners.

As I mentioned in module one, *showing* is necessary in horror to create tension and evoke emotional responses from readers. Fear. Horror. Disgust.

Showing is active, as opposed to passive. This means that a writer uses dialogue, action, description, thoughts and feelings to create scenes of movement, which involve readers in the story by allowing readers to use their imaginations and personal experience.

Before we move on, we'll look at the Dean Koontz scene in a little more detail. We all know what showered looks like, so we can picture showered in our minds. We probably all know what a summery dress looks like and therefore can imagine a summery dress made from yellow silk. While we may never have actually been in a master suite of a mansion, I'm sure most of us can picture one in our minds. With these descriptions, Dean Koontz has engaged our imaginations, got us involved in the story, and allowed us to personalize what is going on. This is *showing*, as opposed to *telling*.

Erika explored the mansion. She found William, the butler, chewing off his fingers.

Apologies to Mr. Koontz for my poor *telling* of his *showing* scene. Hopefully, though, you can see the difference between *showing* and *telling*.

I can't picture the *telling* version in my mind. Again, I'm feeling a "so what?" moment.

While reading an unpublished manuscript today I came across the following sentence:

He grinned, amused.

I thought the addition of *amused* was unnecessary. The writer shows readers that the character is amused. If he wasn't amused, the character would not have grinned. Right? But then the writer *tells* readers that the character is amused. Why? One can only assume that the writer doubts his/her own ability to create pictures in readers' minds and doubts readers ability to use their imaginations. So please be careful that you don't add a *telling* qualifier onto the end of your *showing* text.

Show, don't tell!

He grinned. My interpretation is that the character is amused, especially within the context of the story. The writer didn't have to hit me over the head with a sledgehammer to get his/her point across.

Just a reminder – *showing* is about:

1. Convincing your readers that your fictional world is

real;

2. Making your readers care about the main character and his or her problem;

3. Evoking your readers' emotions; and

4. Allowing your readers to participate and interpret things for themselves.

A final word before you sit down to do my suggested activities.

When you focus on *show, don't tell* and the various genres, you gain an understanding of why *showing* is more powerful than *telling*. Most fictional genres rely on the reader becoming emotionally and psychologically involved in the story. And that occurs when readers are *shown* what is happening, thus enabling them to develop their own opinions and responses to the written word – to use their imaginations.

The reader is encouraged to react to specific scenes in your story, which, of course, have been set up by the writer to achieve a desired response.

In a good novel, regardless of the genre, *showing* from the point of view of the main character should always be foremost in an author's mind.

Now over to you. Have fun with these assignments. Challenge yourself. After you've completed the assignments, it's a good idea to try your *showing* scenes out on your friends, especially your writer friends.

1) I'd like you to rewrite the following *telling* statements to *showing* scenes:

   a)   She was pleased with the gift.

   b)   The dog was wild.

   c)   It was a cold, wet day.

   d)   He was tall.

   e)   He looked surprised.

   f)   The car was old.

   g)   She was unfit.

2) Imagine you've just received a telephone call from a publisher, who wants to publish your latest novel and give you an advance of $40,000. I'd like you to describe this event. But there's a catch. I don't want you to mention the words happy, thrilled, excited, scared or shocked. You can

show happy, thrilled, excited, scared or shocked, but please

don't *tell* these emotions. S*how, don't tell!*

3

Show, Don't Tell and Characters

In each module, I'm going to remind you of the difference between *showing* and *telling*.

Repetition is the key to learning. Think back to when you first learned to walk or ride a bike. Many attempts were needed before you mastered these skills. At times, you probably thought your attempts were hopeless. You kept failing. You also kept trying. And eventually your efforts paid off – you were walking or riding a bike.

Practice and persistence paid off.

The same can be said for writing and a skill like *show, don't tell*. Awareness and repetition are the keys to how I mastered the concept of *show, don't tell*. First, I had to know about *show, don't tell*, then I had to understand the concept. Next, I had to practice. And practice. And practice.

Now you know why I seem to be repeating myself – repeating myself and extending the concept of *show, don't tell*.

Showing is about creating mental pictures in readers' minds. *Showing* is interactive and participatory. *Showing* allows readers to interpret the author's words and therefore become involved in the story. *Showing* lets readers experience the story for themselves, as if they are the main character.

Showing is active. It makes your writing come alive and seem real to your readers. The little details your readers are *shown* stick in their minds because they are involved in interpreting them.

Telling is about advising the readers of facts, conclusions, thereby leaving them no room to participate or experience things for themselves. *Telling* is easily forgotten because it doesn't have the same impact as *showing*. *Telling* is also harder to digest in the first place.

What is the opposite of participation and involvement? Nonparticipation, non-involvement and non-engagement.

Showing means that readers are participating and involved.

Telling means nonparticipation, non-involvement and non-engagement of readers.

The concept of *show, don't tell* is important in character development because *showing* creates mental images in readers' minds. *Showing* makes your characters come alive and seem real to your readers. *Showing* evokes the emotions of readers, making them care about the main character and his/her objectives. *Showing* allows readers to experience the story as if they are the main character.

This example comes from Lynne Pemberton's *Dancing with Shadows*:

It was Jay who broke the silence. "Thanks for coming, Mom." The words came out flat like meat forced through a mincer.

A mist of breath rose, like smoke, out of her open mouth. "It was the least I could do, son, you aint got nobody else."

He wanted to say that he had a few friends, decent men he'd met inside, who were either innocent, misguided or just plain desperate when they'd offended. But he said nothing.

Big sigh. I confess to falling in love with Jay as I read *Dancing With Shadows*. By the time I came to the end of the book, I didn't want to give him up. I wanted to keep spending time with him. I wanted our relationship to continue. I didn't want to lose him.

And that's exactly what Lynne Pemberton wanted when she created Jay. She wanted readers to identify with him, to care about him and his situation. She wanted to elicit readers' emotions. Her intention was to transport readers into Jay's world and keep us there until the very last word.

But what does the above example *show* us? There's some tension between Jay and his mother. Jay's not exactly thrilled to see her and the feeling seems mutual. It appears to be winter. Jay has obviously been in prison. But I get the impression that he's a good person who had a measure of bad luck. He doesn't seem capable of a heinous crime. He has few people in his life. His mother is the only person he can call on when he needs a soft place to fall.

It's been a few years since I read *Dancing With Shadows*, so I don't remember the details. My observations came as a result of reading the above excerpt from the novel.

Lynne Pemberton used dialogue and introspection in the above scene, both of which are aspects of *show, don't tell*. Action is also a useful tool of *show, don't tell*. But the writer deliberately avoided a lot of action in the above excerpt because she wanted to convey the tension between the two characters.

As I write these notes about characters and *show, don't tell*, I'm reminded of the real people in my life. For instance, I met my husband, Rob, through a mutual friend. We were all writers. Rob and I chatted – and discovered that we have a lot in common. Then, over time, we got to know each other better.

Rob told me things about himself. But what Rob *showed* me really had the most impact on me. Rob *showed* me that he's fun, intelligent, talented, honest, caring, hard-working and so on.

Think about it.

A person tells you that she's honest and reliable. But when you arrange to go out to lunch with her, she arrives late because she's been robbing a bank. Are you going to believe that this person is honest and reliable? Of course not.

Or maybe she's just late. Does that make her unreliable? Maybe not the first time. But if she's always late?

Show, don't tell is very much based on real life.

I'm thrilled when Rob *tells* me that he loves me. I'm even happier when he *shows* me.

Actions speak louder than words.

In writing, actions are part of the *showing* technique. Another more subtle type of action is body language.

For instance, a character, Donna, can say that she's honest and reliable but readers won't necessarily believe her.

Readers want proof. Readers want to be *shown*, through Donna's actions, dialogue, thoughts and feelings, that she is honest and reliable. Readers want to make up their own minds, just as we make up our own minds about real people in real life.

Who wants to be told that Jerry is the best guy you're ever going to meet, so you should marry him now? No one I know. Surely, we'd prefer to make up our own minds about Jerry by getting to know him. Jerry can *tell* us things about himself but what he *shows* us through his actions, body language and dialogue has more impact on us.

Back to our fictional Donna. Readers will not believe that Donna is honest and reliable if her body language suggests otherwise.

For example, Donna can't look Simon in the eye or she nervously fidgets with her earring. However, if Donna *shows* readers that she's honest and reliable through her thoughts, actions, body language and dialogue then readers are more likely to believe her.

Believable characters seem real.

Let's consider more examples from best-selling writers.

My favorite novels are usually in the crime and thriller genres. My favorite fictional character is Dr. Alex Cross, created by James Patterson.

Why do I like Dr. Alex Cross?

He's honest, hard working, strong, intelligent, brave, a great dad, believes in family, plays the piano and so on. He also has shortcomings or weaknesses. He's believable.

James Patterson *shows* me Dr. Alex Cross through actions, body language, dialogue, thoughts and feelings.

Here's an example taken from James Patterson's bestseller *Violets are Blue*:

"Kisses," I said. "Hugs too."

Damon and Jannie groaned, but they leaned in close and I wondered how much longer they would be willing to give me hugs and pecks on the cheek. So I took an extra few while I could get them. When the good times come with your kids, you've got to make them last.

Don't you just love Alex Cross? James Patterson creates such a simple scene; one that most of us can relate to and appreciate from our own experiences; one that elicits emotions and makes us care about the main character, Dr. Alex Cross. But there's more to this scene – another important reason for including it. The Dr. Alex Cross novels feature the worse serial killers and horrific crimes imaginable. James Patterson includes a scene like the above example to give readers a break from all the horror and darkness.

Here's an example from *Fifty Shades of Grey* by E. L. James:

There's a knock at the door, and Blonde Number Two enters.

"Mr. Grey, forgive me for interrupting, but your next meeting is in two minutes."

"We're not finished here, Andrea. Please cancel my next meeting."

Andrea hesitates, gaping at him. She appears lost. He turns his head slowly to face her and raises his eyebrows. She flushes bright pink. Oh, good, it's not just me.

By this point in the novel *Fifty Shades of Grey*, the author, E. L. James, has introduced the main character Anastasia Steele and entrepreneur Christian Grey. Seen through the eyes of Anastasia Steele, Christian Grey is young, attractive, successful, a shrewd businessman – to name just a few of his impressive qualities. Readers "see" how Anastasia reacts to Christian, as she describes her meeting with him.

The above scene *shows* how Andrea, Christian's employee, reacts to him. This little scene validates Anastasia's own reactions. Another woman reacts to Christian in much the same way as Anastasia does. In other words, this little scene adds further proof, and therefore believability, to the effect Christian has on women.

E. L. James could have *told* readers that Christian has a powerful effect on women and saved herself a lot of work. But what does "powerful effect on women" mean? How do readers interpret those words and create images in their minds? Who cares, anyway, if we're not experiencing the effect Christian has on the main character? After all, we read for escapism. During this novel, we're living vicariously through Anastasia.

E. L. James chose to *show* the effect Christian has on women, especially the main character, and the end result is incredibly satisfying for readers.

Getting to know the characters and working out what is going on are two of the pleasures readers gain from reading a book.

How to describe a character's physical traits without resorting to *telling* or cliché can be a difficult proposition for writers.

Here is an example from Joe Hill's *Murder Past Midnight*:

"And I'm twenty-five, so that makes you old enough to be my daddy. Isn't that kinky?" She laughed.

He glanced at himself in the mirror. He had the muscled, toned body of a natural athlete – good shoulders, narrow hips, muscular thighs, and clean-cut abs. He had done well as an amateur heavyweight boxer in his youth, before he gave it up to devote himself to being a cop.

Joe Hill *shows* us what Harrington (Harry) Strong looks like, through the eyes of Harry himself. The description seems natural, given the dialogue that comes before it. Harry is reacting to what Angie says and his reaction seems normal. Readers also learn that Harry used to be an amateur heavyweight boxer before he became a cop. The author doesn't *tell* us these details, Harry *shows* us through his interaction with another character. The fact that Harry has a muscled, toned body is believable when readers learn of Harry's previous experience as a boxer and a cop.

Describing other characters is easier for a writer. Still, the best way to describe other characters is to *show* what the main character sees, hears, thinks and feels. Remember that a good author is an invisible author – as if there isn't a writer at all, only the characters.

Here is an example from *The Hunger Games* by Suzanne Collins:

I prop myself up on one elbow. There's enough light in the bedroom to see them. My little sister, Prim, curled up on her side, cocooned in my mother's body, their cheeks pressed together. In sleep, my mother looks younger, still worn but not so beaten-down. Prim's face is as fresh as a raindrop, as lovely as the primrose for which she was named. My mother was very beautiful once, too. Or so they tell me.

The main character, Katniss, *shows* readers what she sees, thinks and feels in relation to her sister, Prim, and her mother. Readers learn a little about Prim and her mother, from Katniss' point of view. Readers also get a glimpse of the loving relationships within this small family unit. *Showing* usually does more than one thing.

As a final note on *show, don't tell* and characters, I want to mention children's books.

In the shorter types of children's books – picture books, easy readers and early chapter books – the word length doesn't allow for much characterization. Only details that are necessary to the plot are included.

I grabbed a copy of my early chapter book *Best Joke Ever* and flicked through the pages. This book contains a lot of *showing* from the point of view of Gary, the main character.

Here is an example of *showing* from *Best Joke Ever*:

Buzz looks at me and snarls, "Didya say somethin'?"

Who me? Gary, who wants to live longer? I shake my head.

With these two lines, I *show* that Buzz is a bully and that Gary is frightened of him. Firstly, Buzz snarls, which reveals his character as not so nice. Secondly, Gary reacts to Buzz with thoughts of wanting to live longer. Thirdly, Gary denies saying anything with a shake of his head. When confronted by Buzz, Gary appears to have lost his voice.

At the end of chapter one, Gary reacts with further

introspection. Readers find out:

I really hate being pushed around. I'm sick of being Gary the loser. For the hundredth time… No, the millionth time, I wish I was a popular kid!

Through the short first chapter, I *show* Gary being pushed around by other school kids and, at the end, Gary reacts to the treatment by wishing that he was popular. Readers know, within the first four pages, who the main character is, what he wants and what stands in his way. Hopefully, by witnessing the bullying Gary has to put up with, readers will be interested and care enough to keep turning the pages. Most of us know what being bullied feels like, so many readers should be able to relate to Gary and his predicament.

I'm going to finish off this chapter with an example from *The Shack* by William P. Young:

March unleashed a torrent of rainfall after an abnormally dry winter. A cold front out of Canada then descended and was held in place by a swirling wind that roared down the Gorge from eastern Oregon. Although spring was surely just around the corner, the god of winter was not about to relinquish its hard-won dominion without a tussle. There was a blanket of new snow in the Cascades, and rain was now freezing on impact with the frigid ground outside the house; enough reason for Mack to snuggle up with a book and a hot cider and wrap up in the warmth of a crackling fire.

I've read many manuscripts from new and emerging writers. Sometimes I'll read a sentence or paragraph in which the character isn't mentioned. It's impossible for the writer to *show* from a character's point of view if the character is missing from the sentence or paragraph – i.e. the story.

For a moment, I thought chapter one of *The Shack* was going to start with a paragraph of *telling* from the point of view of the writer. After all, there was no character mentioned in the first three sentences. But in the fourth sentence, William P. Young made sure that he introduced the character Mack and that he *showed* Mack's reaction to the weather.

By introducing Mack and *showing* his reaction to the weather, William P. Young makes sure that the description of the weather becomes Mack's point of view and not the author's. Mack experiences the weather and so, too, do readers, as if they are there, as if they are in Mack's shoes.

Here we are again. It's time for you to do your homework. The following are the suggested assignments for this module. Have fun and, if you can, please share your work with other writers, who can give you feedback.

1) Do you have a favorite fictional character? Why do you like this character? What are his/her strengths? What are his/her weaknesses? What has the writer done to make this character seem real to you?

2) Pick out a novel. Look through the first chapter or chapters and find two examples of the writer *showing* details about a character. What have you learned?

3) Please *show, don't tell*, using a combination of action, body language, dialogue, thoughts, and feelings, that:

a) Dan is cruel;

b) Megan is uneducated;

c) Sam hates her work; and

d) Lucy is responsible, reliable and honest.

4

Show, Don't Tell – Supplemental

In this module, we're taking a different direction. We're still discussing *show, don't tell* but we're going to stop and review the assignments from previous modules.

As a little background, I originally created this *ultimate writers' guide* as a master class, in which students enrolled, received weekly lessons and sent me their homework assignments for feedback. Needless to say, my time involved in offering feedback made the master class a much more expensive proposition for students than what you paid for this *ultimate writers' guide*. Despite the expense of the master class, I gained a lot of students – so many, in fact, that I had trouble keeping up with the homework assignments. More of my time was spent as a tutor and less and less as a writer. Eventually, I decided to withdraw the master class option and sell *Show, Don't Tell: the Ultimate Writers' Guide* instead.

During the master class, some of my students gave me permission to include their assignments in the lessons, so that others could learn from their exercises and my feedback. Once again, I thank these students for their generosity.

In my opinion, it's important to pause for a moment and *show* you examples of the homework I received from my students at the end of modules 2 and 3. My aim is to help you learn by using actual examples and feedback.

In this module, we're putting *show, don't tell* to practice – quite literally. I plan to *show* you other people's assignments and my feedback, rather than *tell* you more theory.

Below, you'll find a student's answer then, following immediately afterwards in italics, you'll see my comments. Then you'll find another student's answer, followed by my comments in italics, and so on. I've tried to vary my feedback, simply because I get bored saying the same thing over and over again, and I want my comments to be useful, if only to reinforce *show, don't tell* in your minds.

So here are the examples courtesy of my former students:

1) Dan is cruel.

Slowly Dan stubbed out his cigarette on Joanne's left breast. He sneered as she struggled against the gag and chains. "You aren't going anywhere," he said as he pulled out a clump of her hair. "That's for trying to get away."

Tears welled in her eyes.

"I love it when women cry," he told her, anticipating how much more he would love it when he cut off her head.

Goodness. He's horrible! You definitely stirred my emotions. You dragged me into the story. I felt sympathy for Joanne and revulsion for Dan. And I would have kept reading but for the end of the exercise. I got the urge to help Joanne. I wished I could help her. There's no way I'd want to be in her shoes. How awful! This example shows how powerful showing is. You've obviously evoked my emotions, made me care, which means I'm involved in your fictional scene and I'm reacting as if it's real.

Alice was appalled when she saw the condition of the horses. She leaned across the rail with Dan and stared at the ribs that seemed to protrude from the horses' bodies.

"They look in very poor condition, Dan," she said, glancing at him.

A sneer began to emerge from the corner of his mouth. "Nothin' a good feed won't fix."

"But they look as though they've been starved for months."

"I've been busy. They've become a burden. Do you want them or not?"

A good choice of scene to show that Dan is cruel. But be careful; "Alice was appalled" is telling. It's easy to slip into telling, isn't it? The rest of your words create images in my mind and stir my emotions. I'd like to give Dan a good slap. But the first three words made no impact on me. I glossed over them as if they weren't there. I don't know what you mean by "Alice was appalled" and I don't know what you mean by "condition of the horses". If you don't show me, then I don't know. I can't imagine these things, therefore I'm not pulled into your fictional world. If you'd like to change the beginning and send it back to me, I'm happy to look at it again.

A slow grin stretched Dan's thin mouth.

The girl's wailing filled the air at the sight of the limp kitten dangling from his hand.

"I think you're going to need new batteries."

He dropped it at her feet as he strolled away from the park.

This is a good example of showing. Your words created a scene in my mind, with clear images and dialogue. Your words evoked emotional and physical responses from me. I'd wail, too, if I was the girl. My comment means that I'm empathizing and sympathizing with the little girl. It means I care! When I read this scene a second time, it occurred to me that we actually don't know that Dan killed the kitten. I simply assumed it. The rest of his behavior is unfeeling, insensitive – it's cruel. He certainly seemed capable of killing the poor kitten, so I definitely don't like Dan.

2) Megan is uneducated.

"Kin I he'p you, Mister?" Megan asked.

He thrust the medicine jar toward her, clutching at his chest with his other hand, his voice only a hoarse croak. She stared blankly at the marking on the bottle.

Good. The dialogue works well to show that Megan is uneducated. I'd probably have written Mist'r or Mistar or similar. The poor bloke's doomed if he's relying on Megan to help him. Again, you created a nice little scene – easy for me to imagine. Showing drags readers into a story. It involves them, as if they are there. I wanted to know more, which is always a good sign. I like your use of "marking". It's subtle and makes me think. I interpret your words to mean that Megan can't read. In a way, I'm solving a mystery when I interpret your words and mysteries are so very popular. We love them!

Megan chewed on a fingernail. "Who's Shakespeare?" she asked, wishing she hadn't quit school in the eighth grade.

Nice. You probably don't even need the qualifier at the end. This example is simple but effective. I couldn't believe that anyone wouldn't know who Shakespeare is, so your words involved me by getting a reaction from me. I'm reacting as if this scene is real and actually happening. No doubt Megan is uneducated. To be told is one thing, but your showing scene is much more involving and enjoyable. I know which one I prefer.

I handed Megan the list she wanted for her camping trip. "Just look it over and scrub off anything you already have."

She took the list and stared blankly at it. "Can I do this tomorrow?"

"It will only take a second," I said, frowning.

Something was wrong. She looked at me for long seconds, then glanced back at the list.

"I really don't have time now," she said, embarrassed.

Then I understood. Coming from the farm she didn't spend much time at school.

"How about you take it home and show Mum. Then you can ring me tomorrow."

The look of relief on her face told me the answer.

This is another good choice to show me that Megan is uneducated. You've created a nice little scene. But the scene could be written with more oomph. "She said, embarrassed" is still telling. I want to see Megan's embarrassment. I want to feel it, as if I'm the main character. How did Megan react? What are her physical reactions? What does her body language show readers? Also the reader should get more of a feel of Megan's discomfort back at "She looked at me for long seconds...". I would have started her physical embarrassment at the end of that sentence. Show it!

3) Sam hates her work.

Sam slouched so low in her office chair, she was almost lying down.

PASSWORD her computer directed.

F*&KYO* she typed.

PASSWORD EXPIRED ENTER NEW PASSWORD appeared on the screen.

Sam exhaled noisily and thought about it. GETSTUFFED, LEAVING, UPYOURS had also expired. What would best express her mood this month?

P%SS#FF she typed.

If only I could, she thought.

Great. I think Sam needs a new job. Pronto! Her feelings come across loud and clear. I can picture her actions and I sympathize with her. I feel her pain. I've been there myself. Who hasn't? I'm sure many people can relate to this scene. I enjoyed reading your words and working out what was going on with Sam. You can definitely see how showing is more enjoyable and involving than telling.

The alarm rang and Sam inched one leg over the side of her bed. I don't know how I'm going to last one more day at that rotten job, she thought, trying to unstick her eyelids.

It's all I can do to make myself go in every morning. She staggered to the calendar on her desk and counted the days till vacation. Forty-six! I'm gonna die!

Great. I'm sure a lot of people will relate to Sam, especially her thoughts. This is a good example because it creates a real scene in my mind, like a movie. The last sentence is a brilliant touch. I feel so sorry for her. She's wishing her life away. Poor thing. But I also know what it's like to feel as Sam does. How many people work so that they can enjoy their holidays and days off, rather than enjoy the work itself? Tell Sam to get another job – quickly. See, I got involved and I'm reacting to your words as if the scene is real.

Sam rubbed her eyes and looked at the pile of papers reaching an insurmountable height on her desk. She knew it should have been done yesterday, but finding the effort was getting beyond her.

"Something wrong, Sam?" asked her boss as he came to her desk.

"No, Ken, I'm fine."

"Then I want those reports finished and on my desk by twelve."

She took in a deep breath and grabbed the first on the pile. It was as interesting as digging drains.

Yep. I get a definite sense that Sam hates her work. You didn't tell me – I had to work out Sam's feelings for myself. I enjoyed doing so. Her actions speak louder than her words. Readers know how she feels, which is kept from her boss.

Sounds like real life to me! This little scene creates images in my mind, as if I'm

there watching events unfolding. It also creates empathy for the main character. I

can relate to her actions and feelings, which means I'm personalizing the story by

adding my own experiences to your words. I'm sure most of us can relate to Sam's

problem. I love the last sentence.

4) Lucy is responsible, reliable and honest.

Lucy punched in the telephone number, checking off one more item on her To Do Today list.

"It's Lucy," she said when the girl answered. "I want to tell you that that check I gave you yesterday was the wrong amount."

"It was?"

Lucy heard papers rustling.

"Yes. I came home and checked. I owe you forty-nine-ninety-five, not forty-eight-ninety five."

Gosh, she is responsible, reliable and honest. Most people wouldn't bother

for $1. This is a good example of showing. Again, your words create a little movie

in my mind. I can picture what's happening and why. I hear the dialogue and see

the actions. What you've written is believable. I might not have experienced exactly this scene, but I know the various elements that make up the scene, so I can believe in your fictional world from my own experience. When I bring myself to a scene, I'm involved and participating. My final comment has nothing to do with show, don't tell – just writing in general – the repetition of checking, check and checked is a little annoying.

Tom caught her attention as Lucy entered the room. "Hi, Honey, did you book the holid…"

"Done," she said, smiling at him.

"How about the note to school telling them the kids will be away for…"

"Also done."

"And the money to the travel agent?"

She looked smugly at him. "He made a mistake in the cost. Forgot to add a zero and it went our way. I rang him to tell him he was robbing himself. He seemed pleased."

I'd like Lucy to run my household. She seems most efficient. I got a definite sense of her character. She's also organized, efficient, intelligent etc. I also got a sense of the couple's relationship. They appear to have a warm, caring partnership. This scene is nicely done. You got me involved by making me think about your words and interpret them based on my own experiences. Seeing as I made up my own mind, I believe in your fictional world. Isn't it much more interesting and fun to write this showing scene than something like my telling statement? It's definitely much more interesting to read!

It was pelting with rain and I knew the buses were running late by the size of the queues, so I expected Lucy to be late. I was gobsmacked when she turned up in a taxi – Lucy who had to save before getting her leaky shoes mended.

"Sorry!" she said, sticking her head out. "I got held up. I found a wallet in the street, and I had to take it to the police station. It took ages to fill out the paperwork."

That was Lucy all over. The wallet couldn't wait, and I couldn't wait, even though I'm thirteen and presumably I'd have enough sense to sit in the station buffet until she arrived.

This scene is nicely written but its meaning isn't as clear as your other exercises. This scene is easy to imagine. The dialogue is realistic. The scene adds to characterization. But I don't think it's clear that you're showing me Lucy is responsible, reliable and honest. Maybe she's being irresponsible by wasting money on a taxi she can't afford. After all, she has to save before getting her leaky shoes mended. A simple detail can throw readers out of your fictional world and make readers question believability. Plus, what do you mean by "sticking her head out"? I can't picture what Lucy is sticking her head out because you don't mention it. Make sure your meaning is clear. Clarity is most important.

5) The car was old.

He kept his eyes on the road even though the car seemed to rattle when it went over every bump in the road. No power steering here. His fingers were like a death grip on the large steering wheel, but she could see a strange satisfaction in his steely glare. His words – a wonderful example of engineering. Her words – rust bucket.

I love her words at the end. I love the contrast between his words and her words. The contrast is very believable. You're creating the right images in readers' minds. Most of us know that no power steering means old – as do rattles, bumps and large steering wheels. You don't need to tell readers. We can make up our own minds based on our interpretation of your words. And, if in any doubt, your female character makes your meaning quite clear through her own reactions.

This car was born before Grandpa.

Nice and simple. The image created is strong and clear. The word "Grandpa" makes me picture an old man in my mind. Therefore I have no doubt that the car must be old – older than Grandpa.

The upholstery was covered with stains and small tears. She had to slam the door to get it to stay shut. The car smelt of wet dog, so she tried to open the window, only to find that it wouldn't budge. Fortunately the passenger side window opened. She turned the key in the ignition, and was rewarded with an asthmatic cough. On the third attempt, it caught, and growled like a ride-on lawnmower. She decided to check the brakes on the way out, just in case.

Again, another nice scene, creating clear, believable images for your readers. I could picture each aspect of the car as it was mentioned. I could picture each action as the main character interacted with the vehicle. At the end, I was grateful that the main character had the sense to check the brakes. I almost felt myself nodding as I read her decision to check the brakes on the way out. I was right with her, as if I was the main character. I forgot my own world, my own home – I was in the car, in your fictional world. I think we can all relate to this car. We've probably had one ourselves or know someone who had one. Hopefully it's gone to the wrecker's by now.

One of the common denominators I found when reading the homework from my students was clarity – or a lack of clarity. Good *showing* skills mean making sure that what you're trying to *show* your readers is absolutely clear. You want readers to interpret your words and scenes the way you intended. You want your meaning to be unmistakable.

When your readers have to reread a sentence or puzzle over your meaning, or simply feel confusion, you're dragging them from your fictitious world and reminding them that they're reading a book. You ruin their escapism – much like a knock at the front door or the ring of a telephone. These are interruptions that pull readers out of a fictional world and jerk us back to reality.

When you write *Alice was appalled*, you're telling and you're being lazy. You're not even trying. But when you have to think about clear, simple ways to *show* that Alice was appalled, then you're working at creating your best possible writing. You're putting in effort and you're maximizing meaning and clarity. At least that's what readers hope you're doing.

As that fabulous saying goes: practice makes perfect. So if you'd like to do more exercises for practice, here are my suggestions for this module:

1) You've come home from a night out with friends to find that your house has been burgled. *Show* this scene or scenes by using dialogue, thoughts, action, body language and feelings – but avoid actually *telling* how you feel by using words like shocked, angry, violated etc.

2) You're 12 years old and your dog/cat is missing. *Show* this scene or scenes using the above instructions.

5

Show, Don't Tell and Dialogue

We've discussed in previous modules that *showing* dramatizes the events of a plot, that *showing* is like creating a movie inside readers' minds. Readers experience the story as if they're right there, watching and participating. In their minds, they become the main character and therefore experience what the character does.

Human beings process the world through our senses first, then our minds second.

Think about it.

You wake up and notice a tempting aroma wafting down the hallway toward your bedroom. You smell the aroma first, then your mind identifies the source as bacon cooking. Hmmm, I just made myself hungry.

The senses come first then the mind. That's why *showing* is so powerful. It's engages the senses first then the mind.

Telling gives readers the facts, without involving them. Any interpretations or decisions have been made by the writer. Readers are given information, but in a dull, lifeless manner – without action, emotion and sensory detail. The vital ingredients that make readers believe in a story, that make the story come alive are missing.

Before we move on to dialogue, I'd like to make an important point. Over the years, I've been told to be specific about information in my stories. For example, the first reader of one of my manuscripts asked me a question – what breed of dog is Millie?

It's easier for readers to create vivid images in their minds if you're specific about the details.

What make of car? What model? What type of tree? What breed of cat?

Showing is about giving readers enough information for them to create accurate images in their heads, so they can experience a story as if they are there. Where possible, be specific about little details.

Now let's move on to this module's topic: dialogue.

Dialogue is one of the easiest ways to develop fully rounded, life-like characters. By *showing* and not *telling*. Throughout this guide, I've been teaching you that dialogue is part of *showing*, along with action, body language, thoughts and feelings.

How do we get to know people in real life? By talking to them and observing them during our conversations. That's how readers get to know your characters, too. By listening to them and watching their actions, reactions and body language.

Dialogue always has a job to do. Dialogue is never just there to fill space or be clever. Effective dialogue moves the plot forward. It deepens, or layers, characterization. It creates immediacy and intimacy, and it subtly conveys information and emotions capable of sparking reader empathy.

Dialogue allows readers to *see* the conflict between the characters, or between the character and his inner self, just as in real life.

Imagine that you have a problem with your neighbor reading your mail. How would you deal with this problem? You could put something nasty in your mail for your neighbor to find.

But I suspect that your first step will be to talk to your neighbor. If this doesn't work then you'll try other tactics. But whatever happens, you and your neighbor will have further dialogue. The first conversation isn't the end of it. And your dialogue will *show* your conflict and the changing situation.

Let's look at an example of dialogue from Thomas Harris' *The Silence of the Lambs*:

> *"They turn out good rummagers at Quantico," Krendler said.*
>
> *"They don't turn out thieves."*
>
> *"I know that," he said.*
>
> *"Hard to tell."*
>
> *"Drop it."*

Can you feel the conflict growing? Can you feel the tension in the air?

I can.

Thomas Harris used dialogue and pacing to *show* us the conflict between the two characters. When a character (or human) is upset, he or she will speak in short sentences with clipped tones, as *shown* by the above example. He/she won't have long deep thoughts or speak in long involved sentences.

Therefore dialogue is a writer's tool for changing the pacing of a novel. In the above example, readers sense the tension and urgency as the dialogue becomes shorter and heated.

The opposite effect (slowing down a story) can be achieved by allowing the characters to think longer, unhurried thoughts and speak in flowing, sensory-filled sentences.

Here is an example of a main character's unhurried thoughts from *Sacred* by Dennis Lehane:

Human psyches, I knew as I watched her brow furrow and her lips part slightly against the pillow, are so much harder to bandage than human flesh. And thousands of years of study and experience have made it easier to heal the body, but no one has gotten much past square one on the human mind.

When Phil died, his dying swam deep into Angie's mind, happened over and over and over again without stop.

The main character, Patrick Kenzie, is watching his partner, Angie, sleep. While he watches, he thinks about their relationship and the violent events that touched both of their lives. From Patrick's point of view, through his thoughts, readers learn about his relationship with Angie and the murder of Angie's husband. Back-story, which is important to the plot, is being passed on to readers through the thoughts of the main character.

Some of you might argue that the above example looks a lot like *telling*. For anyone in doubt, we'll examine the scene a little further.

Is Dennis Lehane *telling* readers about Patrick's relationship with Angie and the murder of Angie's husband? No, he isn't. The writer, Dennis Lehane, is invisible.

Human psyches, I knew as I watched her brow furrow...

This scene is being *shown* through the eyes, thoughts and feelings of the *I* main character, who happens to be Patrick Kenzie in this particular example. What might appear, at first glance, to be *telling* is actually *showing* because readers are experiencing what the main character sees, thinks and feels, as if they are the main character.

The fact that this scene shares thoughts or observations from the main character's point of view means that the writer is *showing* and *not telling*. Readers learn important information from the perspective of an integral character. Readers are allowed to go inside the character's head to experience his thoughts and feelings. The scene is a change of pace, slowing the story down and giving readers a breather from all the action, excitement and death.

Plot information is being passed on to readers, between spurts of dialogue. Remember that a good story is made up of narrative, dialogue, action, body language, thoughts and feelings. Too much of one thing, unbroken and seemingly unending, reduces readers' enjoyment. Dialogue needs to be broken up by action, thoughts and some narrative.

Internal dialogue or introspection *shows* us what the character is thinking and feeling. It also *shows* us how the character is reacting and changing throughout the novel.

The following is an example of internal dialogue from James Patterson's *Alex Cross, Run*:

That name, Russell, hit me like an electric shock all at once. Could this be the Russell? The same phantom boyfriend we were looking for in the Elizabeth Reilly case? Elizabeth Reilly's kidnapper?

Or was this just some horrible coincidence?

Good dialogue (including internal dialogue) often does more than one job at a time.

The above example from *Alex Cross, Run* shows how Alex Cross reacts to a piece of information. It adds to characterization, making the characters and the situation believable. It also moves the plot forward, reveals conflict and creates questions. Hopefully readers will want these questions answered and, therefore, will continue to turn the pages until the end of this novel.

This is an example of dialogue from the beginning of Thomas Harris' *The Silence of the Lambs*:

"You have a lot of forensics, but no law enforcement background. We look for six years, minimum."

"My father was a Marshal, I know the life."

Crawford smiled a little. "What you do have is a double major in psychology and criminology, and how many summers working in a mental health center – two?"

"Two."

The dialogue gives readers background information in relation to the main character, Clarice Starling. It adds to characterization. At the same time, the dialogue moves the plot forward as readers realize that Clarice's qualifications and her availability add up to her being offered a task involving Hannibal the Cannibal.

As far as dialogue goes, this isn't the most exciting piece I've ever read. However, it's more interesting and involving than Thomas Harris *telling* us the background information.

Let's consider:

Clarice Starling had a lot of experience in forensics but none in law enforcement. For the FBI's Behavioral Science unit, she needed a minimum of six years. But she knew the life – her father was a Marshal. She also had a double major in psychology and criminology, and two summers working in a mental health center.

This isn't a particularly long section of information or narrative. However, when I read it in this *telling* style, I find myself getting bored, glossing over the words and failing to take in the details. Quite frankly, who cares?

Showing is more memorable because it involves readers and creates scenes in their minds. Readers can identify with the main character, putting themselves in that character's shoes, and experience the scene as if it's happening to them.

Be careful about using dialogue to convey chunks of background information or to recap a section of your plot. This is called *info-dumping*.

Hiding information inside dialogue is not only tacky it also makes your characters less believable to readers.

Likewise, never use dialogue to *tell* readers things the characters already know.

For instance, in real life, people don't usually say in dialogue what is already known to the parties. In fictional dialogue, characters should reflect real life and be credible, which means they shouldn't state what is obvious or already known.

Let's imagine a conversation between two robots. One says, *"Because we're robots, we don't know what those humans are thinking."* Our imaginary mechanical character wouldn't say *"because we're robots"*. He would simply say, *"We don't know what those humans are thinking."* After all, they both know that they're robots. They don't need to share this information through dialogue.

The following is an example I like from an episode of

SpongeBob SquarePants. A glowing "Exposition" sign appears over SpongeBob's head as he says, *"And look! Mr. Krabs is back from his vacation!"*

Mr. Krabs has just been dropped off by a bus. He's carrying a suitcase and wearing what can only be described as vacation clothes. SpongeBob doesn't need to state the obvious. Show, don't tell!

Exposition in dialogue feels false and lifeless, and is a clear reminder that you, the writer, are there, making sure that you get information across to readers.

Another clichéd trick is where the bad guy ties up the hero, then explains his/her plans for world domination just before the hero breaks free to thwart those revealed plans.

The easiest rule to follow when creating dialogue is to be sure that your characters are being themselves. If you've truly created realistic people to work with, then you will know when something is out of character, or physically impossible for him/her to achieve.

You will also be able to recognize much faster when your dialogue is not moving in the right direction.

Remember the scene I included in the previous module, which

comes from James Patterson's bestseller *Violets are Blue*:

"Kisses," I said. "Hugs too."

Damon and Jannie groaned, but they leaned in close and I wondered how much longer they would be willing to give me hugs and pecks on the cheek. So I took an extra few while I could get them. When the good times come with your kids, you've got to make them last.

Can you imagine the same character, Dr. Alex Cross, saying something like this?

"Darn those kids. Dirty little beasts. I wish they'd leave me in peace!"

Definitely not!

It's important that dialogue is believable and fits the character.

Dialogue isn't just what we say. It's also what we don't say or how we say it or the context in which we say it.

Have you ever said "yes" when you meant "no"? Have you ever said "yeah, right" in an argument when what you really meant was "don't be stupid, you jerk"? Have you ever said nothing but spoken volumes with your facial expression? Call it sarcasm or white lies. Call it unspoken dialogue or body language.

Consider this example from *Executive Seduction* by Jennifer

Probst:

She sighed. "Everyone is so caught up in the rat race. Complete a degree, make loads of money, support a family." She leaned forward. "We start to forget the feel of sunshine on our face, the salty smell of the ocean, the taste of chocolate. We sleep through the sunrise and ignore the sunset. We don't know how to stand still and enjoy the moment."

A slight frown creased his brow. "You sound like you decided to give up the kind of life most people strive for."

A shadow passed over her face as she fought back the memories. Then she forced a smile.

The dialogue adds to characterization and moves the plot forward. But there is another form of communication – body language. A person may reveal clues to an unspoken agenda or feeling through their physical behavior.

For instance, the fact that *a slight frown creased his brow* suggests that he doesn't approve of the idea of giving up *the kind of life most people strive for.* He doesn't voice his disapproval, his body language hints at it instead. At least, I've interpreted the author's words as *showing* a character's disapproval. I'm participating. I'm involved. I'm personalizing the story as I add my own interpretations.

A shadow passed over her face as she fought back the memories. Then she forced a smile.

The body language *shown* in the above two sentences suggests a hidden feeling, which troubles the character. The fact that she forces a smile implies that the memories are not happy ones.

Everyone loves a secret or a mystery. Readers will want to know more about these memories. That's human nature.

Here's another example of dialogue, simply because I enjoyed reading it. This time from *Bridget Jones's Diary* by Helen Fielding:

Not being a natural liar, I ended up mumbling shamefacedly to Geoffrey, "Fine," at which point he boomed, "So you still haven't got a feller!"

"Bridget! What are we going to do with you!" said Una. "You career girls! I don't know! Can't put it off for ever, you know. Tick-tock-tick-tock."

"Yes. How does a woman manage to get to your age without being married?"

I cringed when I read this little scene. I related to it. I felt Bridget's mortification. Thank goodness I wasn't in her shoes.

This scene *shows* us the problem single girls have when most of their friends are married. It *shows* us how Bridget can be treated as a failure simply for not having a partner. It evokes our emotions, makes us sympathize with the character and involves us in the story. This scene is realistic and believable.

As a final note, I want to mention the bits and pieces that go with dialogue. Spoken words, action, body language, speech tags and thoughts work together for clarity. Spoken words can be ambiguous. Writers often team spoken words with action or body language or speech tags or thoughts to ensure readers know what is going on and how characters are feeling or reacting. Spoken words alone can be misconstrued.

For example:

"I wish you'd jump in the lake."

Am I angry with you? Or do I want you to go for a swim?

I'm not suggesting that you add adverbs such as:

"I wish you'd jump in the lake," I said angrily.

Heavens no! Adverbs should be avoided. Adverbs are telling!

I'm suggesting that you make sure your meaning is always clear by adding action, body language, speech tags and thoughts. In other words, show, don't tell.

For example:

I shook my fist at her and shouted, "I wish you'd jump in the lake."

Yes, that's much clearer. And it only took a few words to make a big difference.

Now we've come to the fun part of this latest module – your assignments.

1) Look through the first three pages of your latest manuscript and pick out a piece of dialogue. Why did you choose dialogue for this particular scene? What are you *showing?* Does the dialogue add to characterization? Does it move the story forward? What else does it do? Does the dialogue sound realistic? Is there anything you can do to improve it?

2) Still looking at the first chapter of your manuscript, can you find any piece of dialogue that adds nothing to the story? Why is it there?

3) (a) Imagine a scene between a husband and wife. They are having a loving moment. Using the elements of dialogue already discussed, please *show* this scene.

(b) Oh no! The atmosphere has changed. The husband and

wife are now angry with each other. Please *show* this

scene.

Now rewrite b) from the point of view of the daughter, using

dialogue, thoughts, emotions, body language etc.

6

Show, Don't Tell and Conflict

We all know by now that *showing* is about creating an image or images in readers' minds, thus enabling them to imagine what is happening as if they are there witnessing the events unfolding. The tools of *showing* are dialogue, action, thoughts, emotions and body language.

Showing involves readers in the story. *Showing* allows readers to conclude things for themselves. For example:

Dan unbuckled his cowhide belt, jerked it from the loops of his jeans and lashed across his son's narrow back. "You dummy," he yelled. "I told you to catch that ball."

I picked the above example at random. It was written by one of my students in response to module 3 – *showing* me that *Dan is cruel.*

After reading the above example, I concluded that Dan overreacts, is abusive and a bad father. He's also impatient and unsympathetic. He has no reason to be angry. So the boy couldn't catch the ball. Big deal! Dan's reaction is over the top.

Now here's a second example of *Dan is cruel* from another student. You'll remember this one from the Supplemental.

A slow grin stretched Dan's thin mouth.

The girl's wailing filled the air at the sight of the limp kitten dangling from his hand. "I think you're going to need new batteries."

He dropped it at her feet as he strolled away from the park.

The writer creates a scene in our minds. We can see and hear what's happening, as if we are there – as if we are the main character. While we're involved in this fictional world, we forget our own.

However, as I explained to this student, I'm not convinced that Dan is cruel. In the first sentence, he grins. Does he grin to befriend the little girl? Is he hoping to calm and reassure her?

And what about his dialogue? Is he gently warning her about her lifeless pet? Maybe he's trying to let her down gently. Sometimes people joke to make light of a bad situation. Or is his behavior something more sinister?

When he drops the kitten at her feet, is he being a good Samaritan by returning her pet to her? When he leaves, is he withdrawing because he hasn't been able to console her?

This leads me to an important point: clarity.

Writing a *showing* scene is more than just adding action, body language, dialogue, thoughts and feelings. You need to ensure that your meaning is absolutely clear – unmistakable.

Your readers are interpreting your words. Leave your reader with no doubt – *Dan is cruel.* There is no other possible alternative.

If your readers aren't sure what a particular scene means or why it's been included, then the scene might as well not be there. It's not adding to the story.

You reduce your readers' enjoyment of your story if you confuse them with a scene. Maybe they get the wrong idea about your character. Maybe they misinterpret what's going on.

No one likes to be wrong or confused.

You don't want readers to stop reading and ask questions, like I did with the above example. When readers have to stop and think about what they've just read, or reread a passage over again to understand it, you drag them from your fictitious world. That's the end of their escapism. You've just reminded them that they're reading a book and not watching events unfold as if they are there, which is one of the main reasons for *showing*.

To make myself perfectly clear, when you *show* readers a scene unfolding, as the writer, clarity must be foremost in your mind. Will readers understand what you're trying to *show* them? Is there any doubt? Are there any other interpretations of the scene? Are there better ways of *showing* what you mean? A better word choice, perhaps?

Your meaning must be clear!

Now onto this module: *show, don't tell* and conflict.

Conflict is the driving force behind all good fiction. Without it, there is no story. The whole point of a story is to *show* the characters in conflict.

I love the following quote from Syd Field:

ALL DRAMA IS CONFLICT. Without conflict you have no action; without action you have no character; without character you have no story; and without story you have no screenplay.

Just for simplicity I'm going to look at the basic plot of a children's book. The main character has a problem to solve and obstacles stand in the way of resolving the problem. This is conflict. The main character attempts to solve the problem. He or she fails. The main character attempts to solve the problem. He or she fails again. The problem usually gets worse or a resolution seems further away after every failed attempt. Again the character tries to solve his or her problem. This is the climax, where things get really bad or seem hopeless. Then, of course, things pick up and the main character achieves his or her goal or solves the problem. The final resolution is always happy in a children's book.

The main character has a goal. Obstacles stand in the way. Therefore the main character is in conflict.

There are two types of conflict – *external* and *internal.*

External conflict is a problem that happens outside of the character or outside of the character's mind.

External conflict is something that is standing between the character and his or her goal. *External* conflict can be other people, animals, weather/natural disaster, lack of time, lack of money, crime, loss of a loved one etc.

For example, Kathy Reich's character Dr. Temperance Brennan is a forensic anthropologist who has the same goal every novel: she investigates human remains at crime scenes where the flesh is too degraded for a coroner to obtain evidence (victims of arson, mutilation, advanced decomposition, etc.). This is *external* conflict – the conflict comes from outside of the character, from an external source.

An *external* conflict must be something that cannot be resolved too easily or avoided. A character has to face his/her problem, with strong motivation leading him/her toward a worthwhile goal/resolution, or there is no story.

A character's problem may change and multiply as the story unfolds but the original goal should be strong enough to remain until it is eventually resolved at the conclusion of your novel.

Internal conflict comes from inside the character.

Internal conflict is emotional or psychological. For example, fear, jealousy, phobias, insecurity, envy etc. *Internal* conflict is often a battle between what a character wants to do and what a character must do.

In the beginning of Fyodor Dostoyevsky's *Crime and Punishment*, the main character is hopelessly in debt and afraid of meeting his landlady. The author describes the character:

This was not because he was cowardly and abject, quite the contrary: but for some time past, he had been in an overstrained, irritable condition, verging on hypochondria. He had become so completely absorbed in himself, and isolated from his fellows that he dreaded meeting, not only his landlady, but anyone at all.

This character is struggling with himself – *internal* conflict. His problems have nothing to do with other people or outside forces. His *internal* conflict is all about him and his fears/feelings.

A good story can, and some say should, include both *external* and *internal* conflicts.

Wherever possible increase the stakes – up the ante – and make things harder for your characters.

How a character reacts to conflict depends on his/her personality, strengths and weaknesses.

Another important factor is the character's motivation, which also depends on his/her personality, background and experiences.

We react differently to things – people, circumstances, problems – depending on who we are. Our personalities, backgrounds and experiences define our reactions.

For instance, a person who has been bitten by a dog will most likely react differently when confronted by a large dog than a person who has never been bitten. This situation would probably put the bite victim in conflict, while the second person is calm and happy.

In regards to motivation, the bite victim will probably be highly motivated to get away from the dog. For the second person, getting away from the dog is probably no big deal. This person might stop to pat the dog, before continuing on his/her way.

A character should learn, grow and change as a result of resolving his or her conflict, whether it is *external* or *internal*. This experience should change him or her for the better.

This *growth* is part of the satisfaction readers gain from reading your book.

Having said all of the above, what does conflict have to do with the concept of *show, don't tell?*

Let me *show* you what I mean. Here's a scene that occurs early in the Alice Sebold best seller *The Lovely Bones*:

"Mr. Harvey, I really have to get home."

"Take off your clothes."

"What?"

"Take your clothes off," Mr. Harvey said. *"I want to check that you're still a virgin."*

"I am, Mr. Harvey," I said.

"I want to make sure. Your parents will thank me."

"My parents?"

"They only want good girls," he said.

"Mr. Harvey," I said, *"please let me leave."*

"You aren't leaving, Susie. You're mine now."

Alice Sebold has *shown* us a scene of conflict. We know that Mr. Harvey, a neighbor, has Susie trapped in an underground clubhouse. We also know that Susie is dead. She was murdered. At this stage, we don't know the circumstances of the crime. In the above scene, we feel the tension and know that Susie is in grave danger. We suspect the murder will soon be upon us. To find out what happens, we have to read on. That's the whole point — Alice Sebold wants us to read on.

The conflict facing Susie is external — outside of her in the form of another person.

The scene is dramatic. The dialogue is short, terse, which we discussed in the previous module creates tension, drama, conflict. Dialogue is a great way to develop conflict.

The lack of action or body language in the above excerpt also creates tension. Too much action would be distracting to readers, and unnecessary, thus reducing the tension. The lack of action and body language is also realistic and believable, given the circumstances.

Now let me rewrite this scene for you. My apologies to Alice Sebold.

I told Mr. Harvey that I had to go home. But he stood in my way and told me to take off my clothes. I was shocked. He explained that he wanted to check that I was still a virgin. I was a virgin and I told him so. He didn't care. He wanted to make sure and said that my parents would thank him. According to Mr. Harvey my parents only wanted good girls. I begged him to let me leave. He told me that I couldn't leave — I was his now.

The same conflict is evident in Alice Sebold's *showing* version and my *telling* version. That is, Mr. Harvey is stopping Susie from leaving and insisting that she take off her clothes. Despite the same storyline, the original version has more impact – a scene is created, complete with clipped dialogue, which involves readers as if they are there witnessing events unfolding. My eyes glossed over the second *telling* version and I didn't really take the words in.

Alice Sebold's novel has a length of 328 pages. How would you feel if you had to read 328 pages of the second *telling* style? In truth, you'd probably put the book down and never read all 328 pages. Thank goodness, Alice Sebold is a talented writer who knows how to *show, don't tell*.

Here's another example of a scene of conflict taken from one of my favorite novels, *The Eagle Has Landed* by Jack Higgins:

"I've already told you, I haven't the slightest idea," he said, looking more hunted still.

And then I remembered something. "You were here in nineteen-forty-three, weren't you? That's when you took over the parish. It says so on the board inside the church."

He exploded, came apart at the seams. "For the last time, will you replace that stone as you found it?"

"No," I said. "I'm afraid I can't do that."

There's no doubting the conflict in the above scene. I haven't included the scene in its entirety because it ran for more than a page.

The conflict is largely *shown* through dialogue. Jack Higgins took care when choosing his words. Father Vereker's discomfort and reluctance to talk is clear through his dialogue. Readers are also *shown* his body language – *looking more hunted still.* A few moments later, readers are *shown* Father Vereker exploding, coming apart at the seams.

What if Jack Higgins used a *telling* style to convey the above conflict? He could have written:

He repeated himself, trying to convince me that he didn't have the slightest idea.

I remembered something and pointed out that he had been at the church in nineteen forty-three. The board inside the church indicated that year as when he'd taken over the parish.

He got even angrier and demanded, for the last time, that I replace the stone.

I told him simply that I couldn't do as he wished.

The conflict is still evident in this *telling* version. We know that the two characters are at odds over something. But, frankly, the second version isn't very interesting. It fails to engage. We have trouble visualizing what's taking place. We don't feel as if we're there watching the scene unfold. It doesn't stir our emotions. In fact, it barely gets a response – thus diluting the conflict.

Why would we want to read on?

The two examples from Alice Sebold and Jack Higgins, or rewriting the two examples, prove that it's imperative to *show* scenes of conflict.

Conflict! The word inspires emotions and reactions.

You want to involve your readers. You want them to care about your characters and their problems. You want them to empathize, sympathize, and many other emotions. You want to stir their senses. You want them to feel and react.

We already know that *showing* involves actions, body language, dialogue, thoughts and feelings. So, when creating your scenes of conflict, these are the tools to use for the best results.

Creating conflict isn't just a matter of adding violence to a story. Remember the examples of *external* and *internal* conflict I mentioned earlier in this module.

Conflict should never rely on coincidences and misunderstandings.

Creating conflict should be as simple as continuing to ask yourself questions during every scene – and then forcing yourself to be honest about the answers.

Ask about the actions of your characters. For example, is your hero reacting in a realistic way to the conflict you have thrown at him? Would he really do that? Remember the character's background, experience and personality affect how he reacts to various situations.

Ask about the continuity. For example, does this scene move the story forward? Is it necessary? What details about the scenery and actions should be included in the story to ensure readers get clear mental images? Does a scene increase or decrease the tension?

But most importantly, ask questions about your readers. Why should readers care what happens to your characters? Why should readers keep turning those pages? Why would readers want to read what happens next?

By now you should know what's coming next. Yes, it's time for you to have some fun.

So, over to you:

1. Write a scene that *shows* a character struggling with an internal conflict.

2. Write a scene that *shows* a character struggling with an external conflict.

Write an opening scene, or a scene that appears early in your novel, which *shows* the essence of what your story is about i.e. a murder, finding a lost dog, a disaster, government conspiracy, conquering a phobia etc.

7

Show, Don't Tell and Plot

Progression

When I read, I picture the events, hear the dialogue and react accordingly – emotionally and physically.

For example, *tell* me that Dan is cruel and I can hardly coax any interest. These three words mean little to me. I don't understand. These words don't evoke an emotional response. They're cold, distant, meaningless. But *show* me that Dan has strangled a cat, and loved every second, and I react strongly with feelings of shock, outrage and revulsion. How dare he! The miserable so-and-so. The poor cat. I understand, too clearly. My feelings inspire physical reactions of shock, outrage and revulsion. I feel tense, angry. I want to jump to action. I feel like strangling Dan. I want to help the cat.

Showing is powerful. So when you want to evoke physical and emotional responses from your readers, *showing* them a scene or scenes is the only way to go. *Showing* is involving – participatory.

Let's move on to this module: *show, don't tell* and plot progression. First of all, what do I mean by plot progression?

I'm talking about moving a story forward, from the very first scene to the very last scene. It's a fabulous journey. No messing about, no wasting time.

Your story should always be moving forward. Otherwise readers may become bored, put your book down and never return to it.

Think of your story as a series of scenes. Each scene should reveal character or move the story forward. In other words, each scene should add something of value to your story. A scene should never exist simply to be clever or fill space. If a scene doesn't add something to your story, you should get rid of it.

This is especially important in children's books, which have a limited number of words.

Let's look at children for a moment.

Children in the 21st Century are sophisticated creatures. They have a lot more options and demands on their time. They also have a far greater life experience than their parents and much better education.

Nowadays, children also have a lot more stuff than their predecessors. Think of the things a child can do with a minimum of fuss. There's a multitude of toys to keep them amused for hours. They can play sport or participate in other energetic activities such as ballet, kickboxing, Scouts, skateboarding etc. It isn't unusual for children to spend hours playing video/computer games or surfing the Internet. They like to hang out with friends and gather at shopping malls. It's impossible to ignore the impact TV, film and DVDs have had on the average life. Maybe, when there's nothing else to do, children can read.

That's a writer's competition. It's pretty daunting.

Luckily for us there are still plenty of children who choose to read.

Books are competing for the same audience as the abovementioned activities. Therefore books have to be just as good, if not better, than those activities.

Many children have been conditioned by TV and film. They are used to watching a story unfold in one hour – three hours at the most. TV shows and films are fast moving, action-packed, because the story is told in a short time frame and, of course, the filmmakers don't want viewers to turn off their televisions.

It takes a lot more time to read a Harry Potter novel than it does to watch the movie.

Nowadays, children are used to experiencing a lot of images and ideas occurring together and changing quickly. This experience influences what we can do in our writing. To be competitive, children's books have to be fast moving and action-packed too.

Modern children's books have more dialogue and lots of action, less description. In some books, description is limited to the characters' movements. Authors are expected to start the story in the middle of the action and end every chapter with a page-turner.

Why am I talking about children and children's books if you're writing for adults?

In truth, adults aren't so different from children. The above logic also applies to adults, though some of the activities are different.

Adults live busy, demanding lives. We don't have a lot of time for recreational activities, and we have a lot of options when we do find time for relaxation or fun. We're used to the fast-pace of television and movies. We like our stories to move forward at an interesting, time-efficient pace.

Imagine watching a movie where the first twenty minutes is just scenery (description) which does nothing more than set the scene. Most of us would leave the cinema or change the TV channel.

Everything that happens in a movie is necessary to the plot. Every scene moves the story forward and keeps the audience interested.

Descriptions need to further the plot i.e. move the story forward. You don't need to explain everything that happens, only what advances the plot or adds to characterization (which is another means of advancing the plot).

Remember the quote from Syd Field that I included in the

previous chapter: *ALL DRAMA IS CONFLICT. Without conflict you have no action; without action you have no character; without character you have no story; and without story you have no screenplay.*

Descriptions of the setting or the weather or other descriptions to set the scene must somehow add to the story, characterization, drama.

Some description is necessary to the story i.e. the setting. The best way to describe relevant, necessary information, like the setting or weather, is through the eyes of your characters.

This is *showing*.

When you describe the setting from the main character's point of view, you're *showing* how the character feels about his/her surroundings, his/her world. *Showing* the setting from the main character's point of view can also add to characterization.

Your descriptions should never seem indulgent – as if the writer is simply enjoying him/herself or as if the writer is feeling pleased with his/her writing.

Let's look at the opening descriptions of Stephenie Meyer's best-seller *Twilight*:

In the Olympic Peninsula of northwest Washington State, a small town named Forks exists under a near-constant cover of clouds. It rains on this inconsequential town more than any other place in the United States of America. It was from this town and its gloomy, omnipresent shade that my mother escaped with me when I was only a few months old. It was in this town that I'd been compelled to spend a month every summer until I was fourteen. That was the year I finally put my foot down; these past three summers…

Stephenie Meyer is setting the scene for us – passing on information. The main character, Bella, describes a town named Forks. Readers learn about a small town named Forks and its cloudy, rainy weather. This description comes from Bella's point of view and isn't very glowing.

Anyone who knows the story of *Twilight* realizes how important this description of Forks is to the story. In Forks, Bella meets Edward Cullen and his family, who are vampires. In modern fiction, vampires generally have a vulnerability to sunlight. In *Twilight*, when a vampire is exposed to sunlight, his/her body will sparkle like diamonds. The fact that the Cullens live in Forks is important. For the majority of the year, Forks is wet, foggy and cloudy. The Cullens exposure to sunlight is limited and this vampire family is able to hide in plain sight.

At the end of the excerpt from *Twilight*, the discerning reader learns that Bella is seventeen. Therefore, the excerpt also adds to characterization.

Description, scene setting, that is important to the story is more interesting when viewed through the eyes and mind of the main character. It's the character readers are interested in. It's his/her story we're reading about. We want to get inside his/her head, share his/her experiences and world, and sometimes we even want to be the character.

In the above excerpt, Stephenie Meyer gives us the opportunity to conclude things for ourselves from the information she is *showing* us. Coming from the perspective of the main character, this information is interesting. It sets the scene and adds to characterization. It moves the story forward.

Your story has a beginning, middle and an end. How's that for a revelation!

Showing establishes who, what, where – then you move the plot

forward.

A friend of mine recently commented that when she's reading a novel with a lot of description, she thinks that the descriptions must be necessary to the plot. She tries to remember all the information contained in the descriptions, assuming that these details have some relevance, which will become clear later on in the novel. Then, sometimes, she discovers that the information has no bearing on the plot at all.

"Why are the descriptions there?" she asks. "Why is the writer telling me these things?"

Good question.

My friend is confused and frustrated when she has to wade through a lot of unnecessary information. She has to decide what's important and what's not. So much for escapism!

Is this what you want – to confuse and frustrate your readers?

Not if you want the same readers to buy your next book and the next and...

Here's an example of *showing* character background information from J. K. Rowling's *Harry Potter and the Sorcerer's Stone:*

The only thing Harry liked about his own appearance was a very thin scar on his forehead that was shaped like a bolt of lightning. He had had it as long as he could remember, and the first question he could ever remember asking his Aunt Petunia was how he had gotten it.

"In the car crash when your parents died," she had said. "And don't ask questions."

Don't ask questions – that was the first rule for a quiet life with the Dursleys.

J. K. Rowling *shows* readers, from Harry's point of view, that he has a very thin scar on his forehead shaped like a bolt of lightning, that the scar is the only thing he likes about his own appearance and that he got the scar in the car crash which killed his parents. *Don't ask questions,* readers also learn, is the first rule for a quiet life with the Dursleys.

Fans of Harry Potter know that the scar on his forehead shaped like a bolt of lightning is important to characterization and the plot. The above excerpt moves the story forward. It has a purpose.

The above excerpt is interesting because initially it might

appear as if the author is *telling* readers about Harry. When a writer shares information with readers from the character's point of view it is a form of *showing*. We're seeing life through the eyes of the character, learning more about him and his world. We become involved in the story. We care about what's going on.

In this instance, readers learn about Harry's appearance from his point of view – what Harry likes, dislikes and how he feels. Readers are privy to Harry's memories and how he reacts to those memories from his point of view.

In the module on characters, I explained that I've read many manuscripts from new and emerging writers and that sometimes I'll come across a sentence or paragraph in which the character isn't mentioned. It's impossible for the writer to *show* from a character's point of view if the character is missing from the sentence or paragraph – i.e. the story. There is no point of view character, only the writer. Therefore the writer is *telling* readers and not *showing* through the eyes and ears of a character.

So, what is necessary to the plot? What should we be *showing* our readers?

Let's look at another example from *The Shack* by William P. Young:

"Now, Annie, you know I don't smoke dope—never did, and don't ever want to." Of course Annie knew no such thing, but Mack was taking no chances on how she might remember the conversation in a day or two. Wouldn't be the first time that her sense of humor morphed into a good story that soon became "fact". He could see his name being added to the church prayer chain. "It's okay, I'll just catch Tony some other time, no big deal."

There are more than 20 million copies of *The Shack* in print, but if you haven't read this book, you have to assume that the above excerpt is necessary to the story. This scene must move the plot forward. Otherwise, why is it in the novel? Why should we, the readers, care? This scene adds to characterization by *showing* how the main character relates to other characters. Perhaps the reference to smoking dope is important to the plot. Either way, there has to be a point to the scene.

This is where a lot of what we've already learned comes together.

Earlier in this book, I explained that dialogue should do one of the following things:

1. *Show* character i.e. add to characterization;

2. Move the story forward i.e. furthers the action of the story;

3. *Show* conflict and tension i.e. clipped dialogue shows conflict between two characters;

4. Pass on necessary information i.e. provide background information on characters and the setting; and/or

5. Create immediacy and intimacy i.e. spark reader empathy.

In the previous module, we looked at conflict.

Conflict is the driving force behind all good fiction. Without it, there is no story. The whole point of a story is to *show* the characters in conflict.

With conflict, you want to involve readers. You want readers to care about your characters and their problems. You want them to empathize, sympathize, and many other emotions. You want to stir their senses.

In other words, every scene in your novel or short story must do something. Just like every person in an office has a job to do.

Ask yourself – does this scene add to characterization? Does it more the story forward?

And the best way to add to characterization or move a story forward is by *showing* your readers – creating scenes in their minds.

Here's another example from *The Da Vinci Code*:

"Who is it?" Fache said.

The agent frowned. "It's the director of our Cryptography Department."

"And?"

"It's about Sophie Neveu, sir. Something is not quite right."

This scene comes at the end of a chapter. It's a page-turner. We've been given enough information to be curious about what happens next. So we turn the page to find out. What isn't *quite right?*

Now imagine that this scene is totally irrelevant to the story. Imagine readers' disappointment when they read on to find out that the scene has nothing to do with the story. It's likely that readers will feel conned or let down. They may never trust the writer again. Luckily Dan Brown wouldn't think of doing such a thing.

When I watched episodes of the TV show *Murder, She Wrote*, I learned that something is only ever mentioned if it's important to the plot. This knowledge makes it easier to pick up the clues and deduce who the murderer is before his or her identity is revealed.

Scenes in *Murder, She Wrote* are all necessary to the story. Every scene moves the story forward from beginning to middle to end. No character is unnecessary.

Your novel should work in the same way.

Show your readers what is happening. But only ever *show* them what is necessary to the story – what moves the characters and plot from beginning to end.

So how does one plot a novel?

First of all you need to know your characters inside and out. After all, it's your characters' conflict, motivation, personality, background, strengths and weaknesses that determine how they react to certain situations.

Remember my example from earlier – when confronted by a large dog, someone who has been bitten by a dog will react differently from someone who has never been bitten.

Remember that you're writing a character's story, so it's the character who determines the plot, not the other way around.

My suggestion is that you take a large piece of paper and write beginning at the top and end at the bottom. Write one line about your opening scene i.e. Laura is finishing her solo at a rehearsal of the school play. Then write one line about your final scene i.e. Laura's parents and teacher come to her rescue.

Fill in the blanks by writing down the major plot points that move your plot forward from the beginning of your novel to the end.

When you're happy with the resultant *plot map*, you can transfer it to your computer and flesh out the single lines, link them together – but never write too much detail. The last thing you want is to feel like you've already written the story and, as a consequence, your interest has waned.

At this stage, you're most likely *telling* yourself what will happen in your story. The *plot map* is a guide to help you decide whether you have a story that can fill 200 pages and is something that other people will want to read. It also prevents you from running out of puff (or ideas) halfway through your novel and giving up on it. With a *plot map*, you have a clear direction of where your story is going and are more likely to finish your novel.

When you come to writing your novel, you want to *show* your readers these scenes, so they can *see* and *hear* what is happening – as if they are there.

During a brainstorming session, I started work on a *plot map*. I took one idea and followed it in many directions. My *plot map* will give you an idea of what you can do.

The link to my *plot map* can be found in an article I wrote about plotting. Scroll down, about three-quarters of the page, to find the following link –

http://www.robynopie.com/articles/writingforchildren_plotti ngachildrensbook.htm

Now it's time for you to do some exercises of your own to put the above information to practice.

1) Look at the first chapter of your manuscript. Write up a plot outline. In other words, write a brief list of the scenes that take place from the first word of the chapter to the last.

2) Still focusing on the first chapter of your manuscript, ask yourself the following questions:

   a) Are you *telling* your readers background information that could be *shown* from the character's point of view? If so, change it.

b) Is all the background information vital for the story to make sense i.e. is it necessary to the plot?

c) Is every scene necessary to the plot?

d) Does the novel move forward quickly, slowly, erratically? Do you need to look at the pace of your novel?

3) Let's now look at chunks of narrative, which are usually descriptive passages of prose. Some narrative is fine and, in some cases, even important to a story. But if it doesn't further the plot it's pointless.

a) Is the description necessary to the plot or character? Remember your readers don't need to know everything a character sees or does.

b) Have you described necessary details from the character's point of view? Or are you *telling* your readers what you want them to know?

c) Are you *telling* your readers what comes next in your story? Or are you *showing* them events unfolding?

If it helps you, you can also look at some of the novels you have at home. Study the way the author shows background information and description. Consider whether every scene in the book is necessary to the plot, thus moving it forward. You can even contemplate whether you'd do things differently.

Have fun!

8

Show, Don't Tell and Short Stories

One of my students asked me a question about back-story. He wanted to know my thoughts on back-story or background information. He'd been told by a mentor to never include back-story in a novel, just action.

Sounds like Bruce's mentor was instructing him to *show, don't tell*.

To include back-story, or not to include back-story: that is the question.

The answer depends on how Bruce handles the back-story. If he *tells* readers the back-story in large chunks of narrative, he's slowing down or interrupting the story. Readers will probably become bored and skim over the details. (I confess to sometimes skipping pages of a novel because I'm trying to find the good bits again – the action.) But if Bruce *shows* readers…

When you *show* the events of your story unfolding, your readers feel as if they are in your fictional world, witnessing the events as they are happening. With *showing*, you allow your readers to picture the scenes in their minds and to participate by forming their own conclusions. Readers believe in your fictional world because they believe in their own conclusions. You, the writer, evoke emotional and physical responses from your readers through carefully created *showing* scenes.

For example, in a horror novel some of the emotions you're hoping to inspire in your readers are horror, disgust and revulsion.

As I've mentioned on several occasions, your readers don't want to read 300 pages of *telling*. The simple lack of involvement will lead to boredom and probably sleep.

Likewise, your readers don't want to read 300 pages of *showing*. They don't want to be emotionally involved in the story the whole time. They don't want to spend the entire 300 pages feeling horror, disgust and revulsion.

Telling allows your readers to rest. It allows your readers to relax their level of concentration and involvement. *Telling* gives readers a little downtime.

There are degrees of *showing*.

The strongest form of *showing* are those scenes that *show* us *Dan is cruel* or *the car is old* or *she was pleased with her gift*.

A more subtle form of *showing* is providing readers with background information or description from a character's point of view.

We learn more about the character and setting when we *see* things through the character's eyes. We *see* how the character feels about himself, as in the earlier excerpt from *Harry Potter and the Sorcerer's Stone*, and how he feels about his environment. We *see* how the character interacts with the world around him. We are drawn into the character's world and life.

As a writer, you want to build a relationship between your readers and your main character. You want your readers to *see* things through the eyes of your main character. Even better, you want your readers to see, hear, touch, taste, smell, think and feel through the senses of your main character. The senses bring a story to life, in the same way as the senses bring the real world to life.

You want readers to empathize and sympathize with your main character. Your readers want the same thing.

Readers like to get inside the head of the main character, to experience the world from his/her point of view. This is escapism. At the time of reading, the character's life is more interesting than our own and, at the same time, simpler because we know that all will end well for the character. Or maybe our life is too interesting, chaotic or problematic and we want to read to escape from our own situations.

When we *show* background information or description, we use the writers' tools of dialogue, action, body language, thoughts and feelings.

In my student's case, the back-story he wanted to introduce was about a previous incident that had left the main character with a phobia.

Back-story is necessary when it comes to explaining something as important as a phobia.

If my student doesn't explain how his character got this phobia, his character won't be believable. Readers won't understand, empathize or sympathize.

A character's motivation and behavior must always be clear and logical. Back-story is often necessary to *show* why a character acts in certain ways. In this case, the phobia is essential to characterization.

Where possible *show* short paragraphs of description and back-story from the character's point of view. Too much description and back-story – huge chunks of narrative – will slow the story down. Keep your paragraphs as brief as possible and only ever *show* your readers what is essential to your story. As we've already discussed, sometimes back-story is essential – but not always.

Remember the earlier example from *Sacred* by Dennis Lehane, which I included in the chapter on *Show, Don't Tell and Dialogue*:

Human psyches, I knew as I watched her brow furrow and her lips part slightly against the pillow, are so much harder to bandage than human flesh. And thousands of years of study and experience have made it easier to heal the body, but no one has gotten much past square one on the human mind.

When Phil died, his dying swam deep into Angie's mind, happened over and over and over again without stop.

Back-story, which is important to the plot, is being passed on to readers through the thoughts of the main character.

Now on to this module about *show, don't tell* and short stories.

Short stories can be a great way to break into the competitive world of fiction publishing.

Novel publishers are more willing to look at work written by a previously published author. Creating a writer's *résumé* that includes published short stories, articles and competition credits can assist you when submitting to publishers.

A good novel will leave a lingering impression on its readers, and so will a good short story.

So how do you make your short stories more effective?

When writing a short story, it's important to keep the following in mind:

Theme

What is your story about? What is the theme?

The definition of theme from the Merriam-Webster online dictionary is *main subject that is being discussed or described in a piece of writing, a movie, etc.*

Theme is the underlying message or statement behind the words.

The following is a short (but definitely not exhaustive) list of themes:

Honesty is the best policy;

Good versus evil;

Love conquers all;

Blood is thicker than water;

Coming of age;

Illusion of power;

Betrayal;

Man versus nature;

And so on…

Get the theme right and your story will have more meaning to your readers. They'll recognize the universal theme and relate to it, which draws them in and involves them in the story.

Snapshot

Your character has a life – or he/she should have a life. This person has a history and will hopefully have a future (that depends on you). Your short story is a snapshot, a moment of his/her life. Only this event is relevant, and it should *show* your underlying theme.

Bang!

Begin your story in the middle of the action, where things change for the character, where he is faced with a conflict. You've probably heard the saying *hook your reader*. This is your chance. Begin your story in the middle of something big.

Don't set the scene. Don't introduce your character with loads of detail. Get straight into the action. Make your readers curious. Make them want to turn the pages. Then you can sprinkle details about character and setting into your short story. But only ever include information that is necessary to the plot.

Characters

Obviously a short story has a limited word count. You, as the writer, have a limited number of words to develop a story. Don't include too many characters.

Each new character you introduce will bring a new dimension to the story, but it can also add unnecessary length. Too many characters can confuse readers and reduce the impact of your theme. Only include characters that are necessary to the plot. In other words, these characters are essential for the story to work and make sense.

When writing a short story, it's probably best to stick to one character's point of view or you risk confusing your readers.

Plot

Remember, earlier in this guide, when I described the basic plot of a children's book. The basic plot of any children's book is that the main character has a problem to solve. This is the conflict. The main character attempts to solve the problem. He/she fails. The main character attempts to solve the problem. He/she fails. The problem usually gets worse or a resolution seems further away after every failed attempt. Again, the character tries to solve his/her problem. This is the climax, where things get really bad or seem hopeless.

Then, of course, things pick up and the main character achieves his/her goal or solves his/her problem. The final resolution is always happy in a children's book.

The plot of a short story can be viewed in a similar way:

1. Opening scenes;

2. The main idea;

3. Obstacles;

4. Overcoming the obstacles;

5. The End.

Description

Again, we need to consider the limited word count. Short stories are akin to children's books. You have limited space to develop a great story. You need to make every word count.

Only include description that is necessary to the plot.

Edit your draft carefully and remove any obsolete words or phrases. Beware of repetition.

It's common, at least in first drafts, for emerging writers to *show* something then *tell* readers immediately afterwards to make sure they get the point. I mentioned this earlier.

Give your readers credit for being able to work things out for themselves. And, if you've shown the scene with clarity, then your readers will get it.

Focus

The more you focus your story, the more your readers will be pulled into the event you are *showing* them. In other words, by limiting other details, such as history, surroundings, other characters, peripheral events, you allow your readers to focus their attention.

Twist

I'm a big fan of surprise endings – the twist in the tail. A lot of my books have surprise endings. These little twists at the tail end can leave a lasting impression on readers. They can make the difference between a good story and a memorable one.

Your aim is to satisfy your readers. So make your ending satisfying, but not too predictable.

Show, Don't Tell

It may seem easier in a short story to *tell* your readers about the events unfolding. Short stories have a limited number of words and *telling* requires fewer words and less effort.

But we know that involving readers in a story necessitates the use of *showing* – creating scenes that readers can picture in their minds.

So far, in this guide, we've looked at *show, don't tell* and characters, dialogue, conflict and plot. All the things we've discussed are relevant to short stories too. Go back to these lessons, reread them and apply the principles to your short stories.

Getting a short story published isn't easy. Publication is largely a matter of persistence. If you've received a rejection for a short story then send it out again. If you've received several rejections for the same short story then maybe it's time for a rewrite.

Are you using *show, don't tell* to your advantage? Are you involving your readers and evoking their emotions?

Another thing to consider when writing short stories is targeting your stories to a particular market. Read what is being published in various magazines. Determine their styles and what the editors are accepting. You can tailor your stories to fit that market or markets.

I've just finished reading a short story by Dick Francis. It's from his collection of short stories *Field of 13*. The story is called *Nightmare*.

Here are two excerpts from it:

(The opening lines)

For three years after his father died Martin Retsov abandoned his chosen profession. To be successful he needed a partner, and partners as skilled as his father were hard to find.

Martin Retsov took stock of his bank book, listed his investments, and decided that with a little useful paid employment to fill the days he could cruise along comfortably in second gear, waiting for life to throw up a suitable replacement.

(From the middle pages)

Johnny Duke looked at the barrel pointing straight at his stomach and turned pale. He swallowed, his larynx making a convulsive movement in his neck, and slowly did as he was told.

"I'll pay back the money," he said anxiously, as Martin Retsov slid onto the seat beside him. The gun was held loosely now, pointing at the floor, but both were aware that this could change.

The opening lines intrigued me. They made me curious. I wanted to read more. And I did.

The opening lines are concise. They set the scene. They pull me immediately into the story.

This story has a nice little twist at the end. I wasn't expecting it. But I won't say any more in case you want to read it.

Then I started another one of Dick Francis' short stories, *Blind Chance.*

(The opening lines)

Arnold Roper whistled breathily while he boiled his kettle and spooned instant ownbrand economy-pack coffee into the old blue souvenir from Brixham. Unmelodic and without rhythm, the whistling was none the less an expression of content — both with things in general, and the immediate prospect ahead. Arnold Roper, as usual, was going to the races: and, as usual, if he had a bet, he would win...

This story starts with a page and a half of narrative. In fact, it's two full pages before the appearance of one line of dialogue.

My apologies to Mr. Francis, but I found my eyes glossing over the words and my mind wandering. I had to go back and reread most of what I'd just read. I didn't get into the story and stopped reading after about 4 pages. I didn't care!

Blind Chance may be a brilliant story – I'm a big fan of Dick Francis' novels. But I wanted to *show* you my experience as a typical reader. Too much *telling*, especially at the beginning of a story, can bore readers to the point that they give up on the story. Getting to the action takes too long.

Think about what works for you when reading. Think about what bothers you when reading. Think about what makes you stop reading. Asking yourself these types of questions is a great way of improving your own writing.

Now it's your turn again. Here are my suggestions for this module:

1) Write a short story of approximately 500 words. This is good practice as it forces you to write concisely and be disciplined. Use the tools of *showing* – dialogue, thoughts,

action, body language and feelings. Make your readers feel as if they're in your fictional world, watching events unfold like a fly on the wall.

2) If you have a short story already written, get it out and ask yourself the following questions:

    a) Am I *showing* events unfolding like scenes in a movie or am I telling my readers that this happened, then this etc?

    b) Am I using the tools of *showing* – dialogue, thoughts, action, body language and feelings?

    c) Is the story a happy mix of *showing* and *telling*?

    d) Does the story start in the middle of the action?

    e) Have I included unnecessary information such as description, setting and back-story?

    f) Am I *showing* necessary description, setting and back-story from the point of view of the main character?

    g) Speaking of characters, are there too many characters? Are all the characters necessary for the plot to work and make sense?

h) Is the plot tight? Does the story stick to the point or does it wander off and include unnecessary scenes?

i) What is the theme of the story?

j) Is there an interesting twist to the story? Is the twist believable or obviously forced by the writer?

k) Is the ending satisfying?

l) Is the story fresh and original? Will it stand out from the crowd?

m) Is the style of the story consistent from start to finish?

Naturally, you can add your own questions to this list.

9

Show, Don't Tell and Editing

We're near the end of this ultimate writers' guide, so, to assist you with your writing, I've prepared a summary of all the important details you've learned about *show, don't tell*. I suggest you copy the list into a Word document and format it to suit your needs, then print it out and stick it somewhere close to your computer. Having these points handy allows you to refer to them at any time.

Show, Don't Tell

- *Showing* draws your readers into your story;

- *Showing* is about creating vivid images in your readers'

minds, so they feel as if they are in your fictional world, watching events unfolding like a fly on the wall;

- *Showing* involves your readers by allowing them to draw their own conclusions from your written words;

- *Showing* evokes your readers' emotions;

- *Showing* is about creating scenes – pictures – in your readers' minds. While a movie Producer uses images to *show* a story, a writer uses words to *show* a story;

- *Showing* uses the writers' tools of dialogue, thoughts, action, body language and feelings;

- *Showing* helps a writer create believable characters. You reveal your characters to your readers by *showing* the characters' actions, body language, dialogue, thoughts and feelings;

- *Showing* evokes readers' empathy and sympathy toward your main character or point of view character. Your readers are inside your character's head, experiencing his/her world from his/her perspective;

- *Showing* also uses the five senses – sight, sound, taste, smell and touch. When you use the five senses in your writing, you're creating vivid, realistic images in your readers' minds. The five senses bring your fictional world to life in the same way as they do in our real world;

- *Showing* background information and description through the main character's point of view involves your readers;

- A good novel is a mixture of showing and telling. Some people say that a good novel is about 85% *showing* and 15% *telling*;

- *Showing* and *telling* affect the pace of a story;

- Use *showing* when you want to add tension to your story;

- When you *show* someone something – when you give him/her evidence – he/she is more likely to believe you;

- When you *tell* someone something – and fail to give him/her evidence – he/she may not believe you;

- *Telling* is about passing information onto your readers, when you don't want to draw them into the story and evoke their emotions;

- *Telling* distances your readers;

- *Telling* allows your readers to relax their concentration and reduce their emotional journey. *Telling* gives your readers a break from the thrills, tension, horror etc. of your novel;

- *Telling* doesn't allow your readers to draw their own conclusions. You, the writer, has made the decision and conclusion for your readers;

- *Telling* is usually the writer intruding on the story. It's the writer's voice, instead of the character's;

- *Telling* stops your readers from getting to know your main character or point of view character and feeling empathy and sympathy for him/her; and

- *Telling* stops your readers from caring.

If you don't understand any of the above statements, I suggest you go back to the beginning of this writers' guide and read all of the modules again. Every one of the above statements has been explained in greater detail within this ultimate writers' guide.

Now onto this module, which focuses on things to consider

when editing your novel or short story.

Grammar

Good grammar is essential. A manuscript with grammatical errors is the mark of a lazy writer or an amateur.

Editors will be put off by a manuscript with annoying grammatical errors and will probably reject your novel on the basis of the first page, before they discover the brilliance of your story.

Remember that publishers receive thousands of manuscripts every week. Editors only have time to read the first few pages of a submission. The competition is tough.

You need to give your manuscript the best possible chance in this competitive industry.

Your aim is to impress the socks off a publisher.

There used to be a time when publishers would buy a raw manuscript and spend a lot of time working with the writer then editing the final work. Most publishers have cut costs in order to increase profits. Editors don't have time to spend weeks or months fixing manuscripts.

If you have problems with grammar then think about taking classes to improve your skills. Another alternative is to pay a professional to correct your manuscript for you.

People read for escapism. As a means of relaxation, or perhaps for an injection of excitement, readers want to escape into a fictitious world. It's difficult to get that *can't put the book down* feeling when you're being irritated by poor grammar and other errors. They're too distracting. Mistakes in a book snap readers out of a fictional world and remind them that they're reading.

Believable Characters

Earlier in this ultimate writers' guide, we discussed the importance of creating believable characters.

Your aim, as a writer, is to involve your readers in your story so they feel as if they're actually in your fictional world, watching events unfold, like a fly on the wall.

The key to creating believable characters is first to know your characters. You have to know your characters before you can reveal them to your readers.

Many writers find it useful to create character biographies. A character biography includes the character's name, age, birth date, star sign, address, birth place, nickname, pets, likes, dislikes, habits, strengths, weaknesses, favorite color and so on.

The more you learn about your characters the better you know them and the easier it is to *show* them to your readers. There's also less chance of you making a mistake by changing a character's appearance during the novel without the appropriate plastic surgery or miracle. Or making a character do something that is completely out of character.

Yes, real people are full of contradictions. But there are usually very good reasons for the contradictions. You must *show* your readers the reasons. It is never enough to *tell* your readers. They may not believe you. They want proof. *Show* them.

Remember that you learn more about a person from what they do, rather than from what they *tell* you. So don't *tell* your readers that Fred is a great bloke – *show* them. Give your readers proof and let your readers come to their own conclusions.

Actions speak louder than words.

Original Plot

A few years ago, I went to a writers' seminar that featured a panel of three editors from different publishing houses. A member of the audience asked the editors what they were looking for in regards to new submissions from new writers. The editors' immediate responses were silence and blank looks passing between them. Finally, one of the editors spoke.

Their unanimous answer was originality, freshness, sparkle, that special something that makes you unique. You.

Every writer approaches a subject from a different angle. Our stories are uniquely influenced by our personalities, background, experience and knowledge.

Two writers can start with the same idea and end up with completely different stories.

You have your own unique voice and style. You are the sparkle in your story. Let yourself go. Have fun. Believe in you.

Fresh, believable characters are a good way to add originality to your plot, as are interesting settings and subplots.

When you write a novel or short story look for ways of making your story fresh and original. Add twists. Do the unexpected. Avoid stereotypes and clichés.

Look for fresh ways of *showing* action and body language.

A story can be fantastic but it must be believable to your readers. Make your story seem possible and plausible by *showing* your readers, giving them proof, and they'll happily come along on a journey with your characters.

I believe that you do your best writing if you write what you love. Or write what you love to read.

Writing should be fun. Yes, it's hard work and often frustrating. So, I guess, writing is hard fun. And I like the sound of that – hard fun!

I think you have more chance of creating a great plot if you write in the genre or genres you love. You should have fun with your plot. I love crime and thrillers. I believe I'd have more fun and therefore be able to create a better plot by writing in these genres.

Show, Don't Tell

Naturally, we've covered a lot on *show, don't tell* in this ultimate writers' guide.

Need I say more?

Well, actually, yes.

You can make your writing stronger by choosing to use active voice over passive voice.

Let's look at an example:

Sue opened the door. (Active voice)

The door was opened by Sue. (Passive voice)

Or worse still:

The door was opened. (Passive voice)

In active voice, the subject acts – the subject performs the verb or action. Sue is the subject in this sentence. Sue does something. Sue opens the door.

In passive voice, the subject is acted on – the subject receives the action. Or, as in the third example, there is no subject at all. Who opened the door?

In another example:

The Managers approved the new policy. (Active)

The new policy was approved by the Managers. (Passive)

The new policy was approved. (Passive)

Passive voice often omits the subject altogether and readers are left wondering. Who did the approving?

You can't *show* from a character's point of view if there isn't a character in your sentence or paragraph.

Passive voice distances your readers.

Passive voice can make your writing flat and uninteresting. It can make sentences sound awkward.

Passive voice is *telling*.

So when editing your manuscript be on the lookout for passive voice and rewrite your sentences to make them active.

Clarity

What do I mean by clarity?

Is your writing clear? Does it make sense? Have you included every piece of information, every detail, necessary to *show* your readers exactly what is going on?

Or have you confused your readers?

Even minor omitted details can be annoying and confusing.

Let's look at an example:

She picked the knife up and wiped the blood off with an old tissue. It wasn't that big but she was overly conscious of it as she walked down the street.

Okay, this isn't my finest writing. Firstly, what wasn't that big? The tissue or the knife? One of the vaguest, most meaningless words in the world is "it" and I try to avoid "it" where possible in preference for a clear, specific word.

Let's presume that I'm talking about the knife when I write "it wasn't that big". So, where is the knife for her to be overly conscious of it? And where is she? Walking down the street at the end but where did she pick up the knife? How did she get to the street, if that's not where she found the knife? Where did she get the old tissue?

I have a lot of questions, which is not good. My questions *show* that I'm confused, that I can't imagine the scene in my mind due to a lack of clarity in the writing, and that I've been ejected from the fictional world.

For us, as writers, thinking that our scenes are all clear and that they make perfect sense is easy. Too easy. We know exactly what's going on. The story is in our imaginations before we write the scenes on paper or computer. We don't need to read every word for our imagined story to make sense.

But our readers do. They don't have our knowledge of the story. They aren't inside our heads or imaginations. They need us to create clear, vivid pictures in their minds or else they can't imagine clearly and vividly what's happening.

Another easy way to confuse your readers is in character identification. Now that wasn't very clear so let me explain.

I'll *show* you with another example:

Pete rubbed the dog then gave him a bone. He took it enthusiastically, running away to the bushes. He went back inside to wash his hands.

Who took what enthusiastically? Who ran to the bushes? But even more confusing is, who went back inside to wash his hands? The dog? What a clever woofer!

Sometimes, when you have two males or females in the same sentence or paragraph, the *he* or *she* identifier isn't clear.

Mary pulled her daughter closer. She wiped the chocolate from her chin.

Did Mary wipe the chocolate from her own chin or her

daughter's chin? Who knows?

She grabbed the chocolate bar she was holding.

How can she grab a chocolate bar she is already holding? Huh?

Okay, my writing is deteriorating. I must stop here. Hopefully, you see my point.

Confusing your readers is never a good thing. Picturing what's going on becomes difficult, perhaps impossible, for your readers. They may have to reread paragraphs or even pages. This confusion ruins their enjoyment of your novel, dragging them from of your fictitious world and reminding them that they're reading a book. Perhaps they'll watch a movie instead.

When I first started writing, I always paid for a professional manuscript assessment from a reputable agency or person before submitting any of my longer children's books. A good assessment will outline a story's strengths and weaknesses. A good assessor will point out silly spelling errors and mistakes.

Nowadays, my editor is my wonderful husband, Rob Parnell.

Research the Market

When your manuscript is ready for submission, you need to decide where to send it. Which publisher or publishers will you target?

I recommend reference books such as *Writer's Market*, *Writers' & Artists' Yearbook* and *Australian Writer's Marketplace*.

For instance, here is the description of the *2013 Writer's Market*: *The 2013 Writer's Market details thousands of publishing opportunities for writers, including listings for book publishers, consumer and trade magazines, contests and awards, literary agents, newspapers, playwriting markets, screenwriting markets. These listings include contact and submission information to help writers get their work published.*

E-books and/or online versions of these resource books are also available.

The Internet has made finding publishers a much easier task. If a publisher has a website, and most of them do, then visit the website. Research what publishers are publishing, and look for submission guidelines. Firstly, does the publisher accept unsolicited manuscripts? Your manuscript is unsolicited if a publisher or editor hasn't requested to read it. In other words, your manuscript is unsolicited if you're sending it to a publisher without their prior knowledge.

Always read a publisher's guidelines and always follow their instructions. Give your manuscript the best chance. If guidelines aren't readily available on a publisher's website, then send them a polite and professional email asking for a copy of their guidelines.

The reason you conduct research on publishers before you submit a manuscript is to save you time and money. There's no point sending your horror novel to a publisher that only publishes romance novels. There's no point sending your children's picture book to a publisher that doesn't publish children's books or picture books. There's no point sending your unsolicited manuscript to a publisher that doesn't accept unsolicited manuscripts.

Be Professional

When you deal with publishers, or anyone associated with the publishing industry, it pays to always be polite, friendly and professional. Publishers are looking for writers who can produce great novels and conduct themselves in a professional manner. They are looking for writers they can work with for the long haul.

I'm sure publishers prefer to deal with professional writers, instead of inconsiderate, demanding, unrealistic, time-wasting people who are more trouble than they're worth.

Make publishers want to deal with you because doing so is always a positive, pleasant experience.

In fact, make everyone want to deal with you because doing so is always a positive, pleasant experience.

Being professional also includes submitting your work in a professional manner. A neatly formatted manuscript, accompanied by a well-written query letter will be more readily accepted than a hand-written, unedited story.

Again, I suggest having your manuscript assessed by a professional assessment agency or person before you send your *baby* to a publisher.

If you want to be a professional writer, you will only submit your work once you're satisfied that it's your very best effort.

10

Show, Don't Tell BONUS!

This *Show, Don't Tell BONUS* was written by Melinda Stanners — writer, reviewer, competition winner, friend and all-round fabulous person.

Melinda and I wanted to give you a reviewer's perspective on what makes a great novel to help you with writing your own great novels. So now it's over to Melinda.

A Reviewer's Perspective: Shooting for Five Stars

I love to read reviews. Film reviews, books reviews, restaurant reviews. I rely on other people's experiences to help me make choices for optimum pleasure, and judging from the ever-growing number of online reviewing sites, it's clear that I'm not alone. In this age of market excess and information access, people want to make informed choices about what they watch, where they go, and what they read, more than ever.

As a reviewer, I approach every new book with enthusiasm. The next book I pick up could be *The Book*, the one that indelibly inscribes that author's name on my recognition radar. The book that shoots said author to the top of my *Must Buy* list, and for whom I would perform incredible feats of strength and daring to hold their next release in my hot little hand.

But what causes such rapture in a reviewer that she spreads this love around to loyal readers? I can't speak for everyone, but to send this little reviewer running to my keyboard in spasms of ecstasy, a story has to contain the following elements:

Strong Characterization

Characters need to be tangible and three-dimensional. I want to know their motivations, their fears, the past hurts that hold them back or drive them on to madness. The entire story should not be devoted to their psychological development, but it's important to show an understanding of your characters in the way that they respond to situations. The protagonist is on a journey, and the way that the character grows and changes on that journey is fundamental both to reader empathy, and the plot itself.

Which brings me to my next point.

Cohesive Plot

Sounds obvious, doesn't it? Surely every story has a plot.

Well, it depends on what you mean by *plot*. A plot is not simply a series of random events that are only held together by the presence of the protagonist. The plot is the novel's raison d'etre. Generally speaking, a good plot contains a beginning, where an issue or problem is revealed; a middle, where the protagonist works to resolve the issue or problem; and an end, where the protagonist either succeeds or fails, and hopefully the issue is resolved one way or another.

You'd be amazed at the number of books that I've read (some

of which I refused to review) that didn't possess a discernible point.

Relevance of Events

I suspect that, at some time in your life, you've read a book that goes into passionate detail about certain events that ultimately have no bearing on the plot itself. The descriptions of these events neither further the plot, nor reveal anything about the character.

Worst of all, they mislead the reader into believing that future events will relate back to these events, leading to confusion when apparently significant happenings vanish like a stone into a lake with nary a ripple.

In fact, with one book that I read for review recently, I stopped attributing any value to anything that the hapless protagonist did, because nothing seemed to relate to any kind of plot or purpose. I grew bored – and believe me, boring your reviewer is bad, but boring your reader is worse.

Relevance of Details

In the same book mentioned above, I started off reading it

word for word. As I read further into the story, I started skimming parts of it. By the final third of the book, I was skipping over whole pages.

What could possibly be so wrong with this book that I bypassed whole pages?

The action was bogged down with details.

This ties into the relevance of events – unless the exact shade of the rose fading from white to pink to a gentle peach pinned to her exquisite pale rose-colored taffeta gown trimmed with 18th century crocheted lace inherited from her poor deceased Grandmother, who died of tuberculosis or consumption as it was called back then ACTUALLY has something to do with characterization or plot development, I for one respectfully don't want to read it. You may have the overwhelming desire to describe in fastidious detail the splendor of their opulent wardrobe, surrounds and family tree, but unless it relates to the plot or the characters, it's only going to slow the story down.

Show, Don't Tell

I want to reiterate what Robyn has already told you: *show, don't tell*. Another book that I reviewed recently told me that John X was a man who was not afraid to tell another man's children to be quiet; this otherwise-engaging book would have gotten a far more favorable rating if the author had shown me John X telling off another man's children.

Consider the appalling example above: If you force your readers to trawl through page after page of such descriptions, you're likely to bore them, and you're taking time away from building rapport with the characters. However, if you consider the information from the characters' points of view, it can provide insights into their personalities, as well as further the plot.

Jennifer admired the sunset hues and fragrant perfume of the rose that Kyan pinned to her gown, and she was glad that she had worn the rose-pink taffeta. Nervously smoothing the ruffled lace at her bodice, the scratchy texture of Grandmother's heirloom soothed her self-consciousness. Oh, how she wished that Gran were here with her now. If only she hadn't fallen ill with consumption… but Kyan was standing in front of her, most assuredly alive, and her heart leapt as he held out his hand and asked her to dance.

Okay, so it's rough, but you can see how tying the objects to the character's psyche give them meaning without distracting from the action. The focus is on Jenna, not the objects, and this change of focus fits much more neatly into the overall flow of the story.

Five-star status is within your grasp, and attention to these five keys will bring you exponentially closer to publication, favorable reviews, and ultimately a loyal readership.

Now it's over to you.

Go write!

More Books by Robyn Opie Parnell

How to Write a Great Children's Book

http://www.amazon.com/Write-GREAT-Childrens-Book-ebook/dp/B00EV5CD14

http://www.amazon.com/How-Write-GREAT-Childrens-Book/dp/0975160923

The Easy Way to Write Picture Books That Sell

http://www.amazon.com/Easy-Write-Picture-Books-That-ebook/dp/B00G1XIUF2

You're Amazing! The Easy Way To Create Your Perfect Life

http://www.amazon.com/Youre-Amazing-Easy-Create-Perfect-ebook/dp/B00FLKJAAU

Maya and the Crystal Skull

http://www.amazon.com/Maya-Crystal-Skull-Robyn-Parnell-ebook/dp/B0069WE3GK

Maya and the Daring Heist

http://www.amazon.com/Maya-Daring-Heist-Crystal-Skull-ebook/dp/B00D3FFUYK

Best Book Ever

http://www.amazon.com/Best-Book-Ever-Robyn-Parnell-ebook/dp/B0071642I2

Best Joke Ever

http://www.amazon.com/Best-Joke-Ever-Robyn-Parnell-ebook/dp/B00A601328

Best Team Wins

http://www.amazon.com/Best-Team-Wins-Robyn-Parnell-ebook/dp/B00FFZ1X4C

Caught in a Cyclone

http://www.amazon.com/Caught-in-a-Cyclone-ebook/dp/B006PC31HQ

Black Baron

http://www.amazon.com/Black-Baron-Robyn-Opie/dp/1406322164

http://www.walkerbooks.com.au/Books/Lightning-Strikes-Black-Baron-9781921150586

Connect with Robyn Opie Parnell

Robyn's Website
http://www.robynopie.com

Robyn's Blog
http://www.robynopie.blogspot.com

Facebook
http://www.facebook.com/robyn.opieparnell.3

Twitter
http://twitter.com/robynopieparnel

Google Plus
http://plus.google.com/u/0/106843754910309370025/

LinkedIn
au.linkedin.com/pub/robyn-opie-parnell/13/829/168/

GoodReads
https://www.goodreads.com/robynopieparnell

Recommended Reading

King, Stephen, *Cujo*, Viking Press, 1981
http://www.stephenking.com/library/novel/cujo.html

Brown, Dan, *Inferno*, Doubleday, 2013
http://www.danbrown.com/inferno/

Martin, George R. R., *Game of Thrones*, Bantam Books, 1996
http://www.georgerrmartin.com/grrm_book/a-game-of-thrones-a-song-of-ice-and-fire-book-one/

Picoult, Jodi, *The Storyteller*, Atria Books, 2013
http://www.jodipicoult.com.au/storyteller.html

Patterson, James, *Four Blind Mice*, Little, Brown and Company, 2002
http://www.jamespatterson.com/books_fourBlindMice.php#.UvR9j
hDyNng

Anderson, Natalie, *Blame It On The Bikini*, Harlequin Mills & Boon,
2013
http://www.natalie-anderson.com/book020.html

Koontz, Dean, *Frankenstein: City of Night*, HarperCollins Publishers
Ltd, 2005
http://www.deankoontz.com/frankenstein-book-two-city-of-night/

Pemberton, Lynne, *Dancing With Shadows*, HarperCollins Publishers
Limited, 1998
http://www.harpercollins.co.uk/authors/4530/lynne-pemberton

Patterson, James, *Violets are Blue*, Little, Brown, 2001
http://www.jamespatterson.com/books_violetsAreBlue.php#.UvV_
shDyNng

James, E. L., *Fifty Shades of Grey*, Random House, 2012
http://www.eljamesauthor.com/books/fifty-shades-of-grey/

Hill, Joe, *Murder Past Midnight*, Origin Books, 2013
http://www.amazon.com/Murder-Past-Midnight-Joe-Hill-ebook/dp/B00G0SFV82

Collins, Suzanne, *The Hunger Games*, Scholastic Inc., 2008
http://www.suzannecollinsbooks.com/the_hunger_games_69765.ht
m

Young, William P., *The Shack*, Windblown Media, 2007
http://www.wmpaulyoung.com/project/the-shack

Harris, Thomas, *The Silence of the Lambs*, St. Martin's Press, 1988
http://www.randomhouse.com/features/thomasharris/

Lehane, Dennis, *Sacred*, Bantam Books, 2006
http://www.dennislehane.com/books/sacred

Patterson James, *Alex Cross, Run*, Grand Central Publishing, 2013
http://www.jamespatterson.com/books_alexCrossRun.php#.UvW
M6BDyNng

Probst, Jennifer, *Executive Seduction*, Cool Gus Publishing, 2013
http://www.jenniferprobst.com/books/executive-seduction/

Fielding, Helen, *Bridget Jones's Diary*, Picador, 1996
http://www.amazon.com/Bridget-Joness-Diary-Helen-Fielding/dp/0141000198

Dostoyevsky, Fyodor, *Crime and Punishment*, The Russian Messenger, 1866
http://www.amazon.com/Crime-Punishment-Dover-Thrift-Editions/dp/0486415872

Sebold, Alice, *The Lovely Bones*, Little, Brown, 2002
http://www.amazon.com/Lovely-Bones-Alice-Sebold/dp/B000FDFVZ6

Higgins, Jack, *The Eagle Has Landed*, Collins, 1975
http://www.amazon.com/The-Eagle-Landed-Liam-Devlin/dp/0425177181

Meyer, Stephenie, *Twilight*, Little, Brown Books for Young Readers, 2005
http://stepheniemeyer.com/gear.html

Rowling, J. K., *Harry Potter and the Sorcerer's Stone*, Bloomsbury, 1997
http://www.jkrowling.com/en_US/#/timeline/harry-potter-and-the-sorcerers-stone/

Brown, Dan, *The Da Vinci Code*, Doubleday, 2003
http://www.danbrown.com/the-davinci-code/

ABOUT THE AUTHOR

When Robyn was fifteen, her English teacher told her, 'You should be a writer.' At the time, Robyn hadn't thought about people writing the books she loved. She only thought about the characters and their stories. After hearing her English teacher's words, she went home and wrote a novel for children. Robyn's first children's books were published in 1999. She is now the author of ninety-four books for children and adults, as well as three feature film screenplays. Robyn is married to writer Rob Parnell. They share their home with Wally the dog, Jessie the cat, and thousands of books on a myriad of subjects.

CPSIA information can be obtained
at www.ICGtesting.com
Printed in the USA
LVHW041527110419
613828LV00004B/816